Edy was a Lady

By the same author

Sinbad and the Wizard Eagle and other stories from the World of Music

Famous Children Series – the childhood of the great composers

Bach

Beethoven

Brahms

Chopin

Handel

Haydn

Mozart

Schubert

Schumann

Tchaikovsky

For Gillian
i hope you will soon be
dancing again!

Edy was a Lady

With best wishes.

Ann Rachlin
2011

Ann Rachlin

Matador
9 Priory Buisness Park
Kibworth Beauchamp
Leicester LE8 0RX UK
Tel: (+44) 116 279 2299
Fax: (+44) 116 279 2277
Email: books@troubador.co.uk
Web: www.troubador.co.uk/matador

ISBN 9781 780880 129 (SB)
978 1848768 055 (HB)

British Library Cataloguing in Publication Data.
A catalogue record for this book is available from the British Library.

Typeset in 11pt Adobe Garamond Pro by Troubador Publishing Ltd, Leicester, UK

Matador is an imprint of Troubador Publishing Ltd

For Iain Kerr
No truer friend or more loyal companion ever existed!
With grateful thanks for the love, patience and kindness
you have shown to all three of us
Ellen, Edy and me!

Contents

1. Edith Geraldine Ailsa Craig

1869-1947

Illustrations

SOURCES AND ACKNOWLEDGEMENTS

1. Frontispiece EDITH GERALDINE AILSA CRAIG, 19th Century. Guy Little Collection. Copyright © V&A Images/Victoria and Albert Museum.
2. Ellen Terry and Edith Craig "on stage" Lyceum Theatre in *Henry VIII*. By kind permission of The National Trust.
3. and book cover Edith Craig and Vera Holme, Barn Theatre, Smallhythe. Painting by Clare Atwood. Photograph by Peter Mould. By kind permission of The National Trust.
4. Ellen Terry and Edith Craig "off stage". By kind permission of The National Trust.
5. Vera Holme 1909. Bath in Time – Bath Central Library Collection.
6. Vera Holme driving Mrs Pankhurst with Edith Craig. © Bettmann/CORBIS.
7. Vera Holme, Evelina Haverfield (seated) and friend c1916. Courtesy Mary Evans Picture Library / The Women's Library.
8. *Found Drowned* Oil on canvas. ca. 1848-50 G.F. Watts (1817-1904). © Trustees of the Watts Gallery, Compton, Surrey, UK/ The Bridgeman Art Library.
9. Mrs. Elisabeth Rumball (Boo) By kind permission of The National Trust.
10. Sir Johnston Forbes Robertson – Hulton Archive/Getty Images.
11. Holloway Jail.
12. "Look Daggers" Edith Craig c1874. By kind permission of The National Trust.
13. Walter Crane illustration for *The Frog Prince* 1874 © Blue Lantern Studio/ CORBIS ART.
14. Actor Fred Terry (1863 - 1933), in the play *Sweet Nell Of Old Drury*, at the Haymarket Theatre. London, 30 August 1900. Playwright: Paul Kester Hulton Archive/Getty Images.
15. *Carnation, Lily, Lily, Rose* No.1615 by John Singer Sargent © Tate Gallery.
16. *Sadness* (Ellen Terry) Photograph by Julia Margaret Cameron 1864. By kind permission of The National Trust.

17. *Tennyson Reading* by Helen Allingham (1848-1926) Courtesy of Burgh House and Hampstead Museum.

18. Interior of St Paul's Church, Winlaton. Photo by Iain Kerr.

19. Marie Corelli and her gondolier on the River Avon. Zazzle Custom Cards.

20. Teddy, Ellen and Edy 1886. Photo by Frederick Hollyer/Hulton Archive/Getty Images.

21. "A nose like Ally Sloper" drawing courtesy Chris Harris.

22. Edward Gordon Craig (1872-1966) as Joey, the Gardening Boy in W.G. Wills' *Eugene Aram* at the Lyceum Theatre, 1885, photo Window & Grove, Guy Little Theatrical Photographs, Copyright © V&A Images/Victoria and Albert Museum.

23. Ellen Terry as Olivia and Henry Irving as Dr Primrose in *Olivia* at the Lyceum Theatre, photo Window & Grove. London, England, 1885 © V&A Images/Victoria and Albert Museum.

24. John Drew and Ada Rehan in *Railroad of Love* Daly's Theatre, Image ID: TH-45381 Original by Von Schoenthan of Tadelburg, Adapted by Augustin Daly, Billy Rose Theatre Collection, New York Public Library.

25. Clara Morris (1848-1925) Image ID: 9947 as Evadne from The Pageant of America Collection at New York Public Library.

26. Josef Hofmann as child prodigy © Everett Collection/Rex Features.

27. Edward Gordon Craig as Arthur St.Valery in *The Dead Heart*. London, 1889, Image ID: 2009BX7294-01 Copyright © V&A Images — All rights reserved.

28. Edith Craig in *Liberty Hall* December 3rd,1892 Sepia photograph of Maude Millett as Amy Chilworth, Ben Webster as Hon. Gerald Harringay, Edith Craig as Miss Hickson, Edward Righton as William Todman, H.H. Vincent as Mr J. Briginshaw and possibly Alfred Holles as Mr Hickson in *Liberty Hall*, St James' Theatre. Guy Little Collection © V&A Images — All rights reserved.

29. Maude Millett (Mrs Tennant) (1867-1920), the English actress c1900. Photo by Popperfoto/Getty Images.

30. Eugene Sandow, ca.1900: performing strongman with a selection of weights and dumbbells. Photo by Rischgitz/Getty Images.

47. Edith Craig in *The Dead Heart*, 19th Century. Guy Little Collection. Copyright © V&A Images – All rights reserved.
48. Kyrle Bellew (1855-1911) ca. 1875-1911 photo by Sarony of New York, Billy Rose Collection, New York Public Library.
49. Ellen Terry as Hiordis in Ibsen's *The Vikings of Helgeland* 1903. By kind permission of The National Trust.
50. Mrs Cora Brown Potter. Photographer Charles, Charlotte 'Lallie', Guy Little Collection. Copyright © V&A Images – All rights reserved.
51. Mrs Brown Potter as Peggy in *Nicandra* at the Avenue Theatre, 1901. Artist/Maker: Langfier, Louis Saul (photographers) Bequeathed by Guy Little, Copyright © V&A Images – All rights reserved.
52. Photographic portrait of George Bernard Shaw 1927 Bettmann Collection © Bettmann/CORBIS.
53. *Pinkie and the Fairies* 1909.
54. Women's Freedom League Social History, Suffragettes, circa 1910. A campaign caravan for the Women's Suffragette Freedom League in Tunbridge Wells, Kent, with two campaigners pictured. Photo by Bob Thomas/Popperfoto/Getty Images.
55. Portrait of Sir Thomas Beecham by Emu from 1917. Photographer Michael Nicholson; © Michael Nicholson/Corbis.
56. Queen Alexandra (1844-1925), Queen-consort of British monarch Edward VII (1841-1910), with her pet dog. Photo by W. & D. Downey/ Getty Images.
57. Edith Craig and Dame Ellen Terry on the day of Ellen's Investiture 1925. Guy Little Collection. Copyright © V&A Images – All rights reserved.
58. Ellen Terry's last role on stage as Nurse in *Romeo & Juliet* Lyric Theatre 1919. By kind permission of The National Trust.
59. Ellen Terry's funeral 24th July 1928: The coffin of English actress Dame Ellen Terry is carried by mourners from her house (background) to the church in the village of Smallhythe. Photo by London Express/Getty Images.
60. The Casket containing the ashes of Ellen Terry in the actors' church, St Paul's Covent Garden, London. By kind permission of The National Trust.
61. Visiting Edy at home in Smallhythe, Vera 'Jacko' Holme, Jack Holme, Clare Atwood, Edy Craig. By kind permission of The National Trust.

Acknowledgements

First and foremost, to Sir Michael Holroyd for his encouragement throughout the writing of this book. I am indebted to him for his expertise and guidance – and for receiving me with warm friendship.

Among the many people who have given me advice, support and assistance, my thanks go to

Sir Donald Sinden, who knew and visited 'Chris' and 'Tony' and kindly made time to read my manuscript and comment on it.

The University of Durham, Martyn Chamberlain, Master of Grey College and Henry Dyson for offering me the Holgate Fellowship and for providing me with the space, peace and quiet to enable me to give Edy's memoirs the concentration they deserved. Professor Alan Martin and my many friends and fellow members of the Senior Common Room for inspiring the lecture "Edy was a Lady" and giving me the opportunity to present it. Paulina Lubacz, Treasurer of The University of Durham for her wise guidance and friendship.

Dick Fiddy of the British Film Institute for his invaluable help in unearthing the silent movies of Ellen and Edy, enabling me to see them acting together on the silver screen.

Gillian Best for her unfailing assistance in times of urgency. William J. Best, BSc, DipEd, CPhys, MInstP, MIOA of the University of Durham for proof reading; Dr. Katharine Cockin at the University of Hull; Chris Harris for providing the history and image of Ally Sloper; Michael Kilgarriff, editor of First Knight, Irving Society; Susannah Mayor, archivist at the Ellen Terry Museum in

Smallhythe, Kent; Paul Meredith, curator and Maurice Dalton at Smallhythe Place; Peter Mould, actor/photographer not only for his assistance with the photography of the two paintings by Clare Atwood at the Ellen Terry Museum, but also for unwittingly reminding me that I owned Edy's memoirs, thus giving me the impetus to transcribe them and write this book!; Annabel Watts.

Dan Brown of Bath in Time; Charlotte Heyman at Bridgemans; Rebecca Lodge at Burgh House; Junez Ali at Corbis; Kate Maconachy and Angela Haines at Getty Images; Mark Vivian, at Mary Evans Picture Library; Laura Mulholland, Special Collections Division, University of Washington Libraries; Miranda McLaughlan at V&A Images Victoria & Albert Museum, London; Thomas Lisanti, Permissions Manager, Premium Services, The New York Public Library; The Women's Library, London Metropolitan University, Papers of Vera (Jack) Holme ref: 7VJH for permission to print Jacko's letter to Curlington and to The Society of Authors, on behalf of the Estate of Bernard Shaw for permission to print Shaw's description of Miss Proserpine Garnett from "Candida".

Special Acknowledgements and grateful thanks to
my three children Jan, Trisha and Max Ziff for always being there to spur me on.

my son-in-law Allan Davidson who never failed to find time to help me with the IT side of my audio-visual lectures and the quirks of my computer.

my faithful wire-haired fox terrier, Sherri who sat patiently at my side throughout the three year creation of this book but sadly did not live to see it published and
Iain Kerr to whom this book is dedicated.

Above all, my thanks go to Edy – who decided in her last years that her memories were worth dictating – and to 'Jacko', her painstaking secretary.

2. On Stage
Ellen Terry and Edith Craig
Henry VIII Lyceum Theatre 1892

Foreword

by MICHAEL HOLROYD

"Gordon Craig has made himself the most famous producer in Europe by dint of never producing anything," wrote Bernard Shaw, "while Edith Craig remains the most obscure by dint of producing everything." Her career as an actress, costumier and theatre director was put in the shade not only by the legendary reputation of her brother, but also by the enduring fame of her mother. After Ellen Terry's death in the summer of 1928, Edy became a custodian of the sacred flame in Ellen's home at Smallhythe "preserving the memorials of our much loved Ellen Terry, not only for those who loved her," wrote the dramatist Clothilde Graves, "but for generations of playgoers and lovers yet to be born". Partly because the last twenty years of her life were devoted to the memory of her mother, Edy never seemed to emerge from this maternal shadow and did not receive "the public recognition that was her due," wrote Margaret Webster in a passage which, written shortly after Edy's death in 1947, Ann Rachlin uses as a coda at the end of this book.

But during the last two decades several feminist critics and theatre historians have been bringing Edy's achievements to light. Foremost among them is Dr Katharine Cockin of Hull University whose recent database on Ellen Terry and Edy Craig together with her scholarly book on Edy's Pioneer Players have done much to give her the public recognition she deserves. It is not surprising that this material has enabled one specialist in the theory and history of directing, the Italian scholar Dr Roberta Gandolfi, to argue that Edy's vibrant and radical staging of European plays on a small scale complements her brother's modernist large-scale visionary productions.

Yet Edy's versatile life has to some extent remained mysterious. And this is one reason why these pages of hitherto unpublished memoirs and autobiography are so welcome. It is not that they are devastatingly indiscreet – there is no mention of the talented musician, Martin Shaw, to whom she was at one time engaged and no indication of her close, volcanic relationship with Christopher St John. These intermittent pages, linked with some explanatory passages by the editor and with quotations from Ellen Terry's memoirs, are spontaneous, direct, informal, often charming and full of fun. Their value lies in the fact that they are Edy's spoken words and they bring her close to us – as if we can hear her talking in the next room. What we hear and come to understand is Edy's shyness at smart social events in company with her mother ("I was glad of the darkness," she writes of one such event at Marlborough House with Queen Alexandra). We can also feel her anxieties when acting on stage: "I was awfully nervous", she writes when playing a leading part in some amateur theatricals in New York. She was to compensate for these difficulties and overcome them with her commanding confidence as a director (which Virginia Woolf described in her last novel *Between the Acts*); and also with her quick discerning eye as a costumier (many of her vivid pen portraits in these memoirs are essentially descriptions of what people were wearing).

Edy is a paradoxical character in the sense that she is most present when invisible and working behind the scenes or at rehearsals. Ann Rachlin becomes, as it were, her sympathetic director and costumier in these pages, transcribing, deciphering and arranging the memories - and presenting them chronologically. Edy had a sharp but innocent eye and a sensitive but mischievous personality. We witness her inevitable falling in love with the theatre, follow her in her travels to the United States and Canada, Paris and Bruges, and are given many emphatic glimpses of actors and writers – including Sarah Bernhardt and Lillie Langtry, J. M. Barrie and Robert Browning. We see Edy listening to Bram Stoker reading from his *Dracula* and learn from her keen observations the arresting technique of Yvette Guilbert, the cabaret singer. Throughout her reminiscences, deftly inserted among some amusing anecdotes, are comments about theatre technique ranging from the dramatic use of supers to the particular needs of singers as opposed to actors in plays. ("I was very anxious that she should make a slow exit singing. [But] the moment she made a movement and took her eyes off Beecham, she went to pieces.")

Edy was a Lady will appeal to anyone interested in the theatre: actors, directors, playwrights, critics and also audiences.

A Message From
Sir Donald Sinden CBE

"YOUR BOOK IS A SHEER DELIGHT"

When I became a resident on the Isle of Oxney in 1953, I thought I had arrived in a theatrical Valhalla. Harcourt Williams lived round the corner, Laurence Irving in Wittersham, Phyllis Nielsen Terry in Appledore and across the field was Smallhythe, where the curator of The Ellen Terry Museum was Olive Terry (Chaplin), to which I became a regular visitor.

Christopher St John had recently gone into a Tenterden nursing home where I visited her and heard her memories of "NELL" and where she eventually died.

Some time later Olive told me that in a "box of my treasures" she had found a box containing Edy Craig's ashes which Edy had requested should be buried "with Kit and Tony" (Christopher and Clare) "when the time comes". When the time came she (Olive) had quite forgotten.

"So what did you do?" I asked.

"Oh, I popped across the road to the Church and scattered them on the graves of the other two."

We are all grateful to Ann Rachlin who caused a memorial stone to be erected in the space between the other two.

Dear self-effacing Edy Craig, the daughter of the great Ellen Terry who was Henry Irving's beautiful leading lady for twenty plus years; sister of one of the most influential figures in the theatre, the artist and stage designer Gordon Craig CH.

Edy lived her life in their shadow and when she died, she bequeathed the beautiful houses that she shared with her Mother and her two lesbian lovers (to the National Trust).

Edy had dictated her memoirs but they remained unpublished until now when Ann Rachlin has performed a labour of love and brought them forth for our delectation.

What a joy they are and what a fascinating read!

Sir Donald Sinden CBE   June 2011.

"I love Edy even better than you.
I think I love her even better than me!"
Ellen Terry to George Bernard Shaw

THE SCENE: THE ELLEN TERRY BARN THEATRE, SMALLHYTHE, KENT

3. VERA HOLME (Jacko) taking dictation from EDITH CRAIG
Painted by Clare Atwood in 1939, Edith Craig, daughter of the great Victorian actress, Ellen Terry, is shown making props, seated on the stage of the Ellen Terry Barn Theatre at her home in Smallhythe, Kent, which she dedicated to the memory of her famous mother. Halfway up the ladder is the actor Charles Staite, adding drapes to the set under Edy's strict supervision. The severe-looking woman at the forefront of the picture is Vera Holme, known as 'Jacko'. She appears to be taking notes from Edith Craig.

Jacko is the link to Edith Craig's memoirs.

4. Off stage
Ellen Terry and Edith Craig

Behind The Scenes

AUTHOR'S NOTES

Dame Ellen Terry, one of England's greatest actresses, died in 1928 aged 81. Adored by the nation, an icon of her time, the public expected her to be accorded the same honour as Sir Henry Irving – burial in Westminster Abbey. Because of her unusual lifestyle and past social transgressions, this final accolade was denied her. Indeed it took thirteen months for the Church to permit her ashes to rest in a chalice in the actors' church, St Paul's Covent Garden. Four years after her death, a new edition of her memoirs, annotated by Edith Craig and her partner Christopher St John, was published. Perhaps it was the importance of her mother's memoirs that made Edy realise that she too had led a fascinating life and had an important story to tell. She decided to preserve in writing her recollections of life with Ellen Terry and Henry Irving, and reveal some of her personal experiences as Ellen Terry's daughter. Now over sixty, Edy realised that her painful arthritic hands (and her poor spelling of which she was always ashamed) meant she could not write down her memoirs herself. So she chose her reliable and trustworthy friend, Vera Holme, known as 'Jacko', to be her amanuensis. I surmise that Edy began dictating the memoirs in 1933/4 and then revised them shortly before she died in 1947. (See additional note referring to the Second World War in Chapter Two) This book contains all the reminiscences dictated by Edith Craig and written down in the minuscule handwriting of Vera 'Jacko' Holme. Jacko was also no good at spelling. It could not have been easy for her. Edy obviously dictated at speed and the anecdotes were in any order, just as they came into her head. I first had to transcribe them, in many cases having to research extensively to try and decipher the place and proper names so often misspelt by Vera Holme. I have at times substituted the correct spelling as there was nothing to be served by leaving the original errors made by the amanuensis.

I am sure Edy would have wanted the words to be spelt correctly. In some special cases I have left the original with [sic].

WHO WAS JACKO?

5. Vera 'Jacko' Holme 1909

Christopher St John, (born Christabel Marshall) Edy's partner for over 40 years, described Edy's last professional engagement and Jacko's immense contribution. It happened in July 1946, eight months before Edy died, during a disastrous dress rehearsal of the Chilham Pageant, when as director, Edy had to re-think the entire production. Like a female Napoleon, she began dictating orders to every department involved in the pageant. Jacko was her invaluable assistant.

CHRIS *"Fortunately for our Boney, she had a loyal and efficient Chief of Staff in Vera Holme, who had worked under her in the Mount Grace pageant and other productions. Our friendship with V.H. (known as "Old Jacko" in our circle where everyone who joined it was sooner or later awarded a nickname), formed in the days of the militant Suffrage movement, had proved a blessing to us in many of the vicissitudes of our lives, but I doubt if Edy had ever found it a greater one than at Chilham."*

Born in 1881, daughter of a Lancashire timber merchant, Vera Holme's interest in the theatre began when she joined the D'Oyly Carte Opera Company in 1906 and became a member of the Actresses' Franchise League in 1908. It was at this time that she also became a member of the Women's Social and Political Union (WSPU) where she participated in the propaganda for Women's Suffrage in many ways, including giving lectures illustrated by a slide show.

In 1909 Vera was one of nine riders sent to greet prisoners on their release from Holloway. Whenever there were demonstrations, she worked as a mounted marshal and also acted in Cicely Hamilton's *Pageant of Great Women* playing the part of Hannah Snell (1723-1792), the woman who dressed as a man, joined the Royal Marines, travelled to India and fought at the battle of Pondicherry. In August 1909 Vera became the chauffeur to the Pankhursts, with whom she often stayed.

In 1914 at the outbreak of the First World War, Vera joined the Women's Volunteer Reserve achieving the rank of Major. One of her main contributions was to deliver a report on the situation of the Serbian army on the Rumanian front to Lord Cecil at the Foreign Office.

Jacko's niece, from whom I purchased the notebook of Edith Craig's reminiscences in 1978, informed me that Vera Holme was taken prisoner of war in Serbia when she was serving with Dr. Elsie Inglis in the Scottish Women's Hospital Unit. Vera Holme's life-long partner was Evelina Haverfield who also worked on Dr. Inglis's team that included Cicely Hamilton.

Although the War Office representative in Scotland opposed the idea, Dr. Elsie Inglis and her Scottish Women's Hospitals Committee sent the first women's

6. Vera Holme driving Mrs. Pankhurst with Edy Craig

medical unit to France three months after the war started. In April 1915 Elsie Inglis took a group of women including Vera Holme to Serbia on the Balkan Front, where the Scottish Women's Hospital Unit established an Auxiliary Hospital with 200 beds in the 13th century Royaumont Abbey. Inglis's team included Evelina Haverfield, Ishbel Ross and Cicely Hamilton. Over the next few months they established field hospitals, dressing stations, fever hospitals and clinics. One government official, who saw the doctors and nurses working in Russia, remarked:

"No wonder England is a great country if the women are like that."

7. Vera Holme, Evelina Haverfield (seated) and friend 1916

Prologue

The Scene – The bedroom of Sarah and Ben Terry
24 Caversham Road, Kentish Town, London
The Time – An early morning in mid-October 1868

Sarah and Ben Terry were not asleep. How could they sleep? It was October 1868 and several days since their actress daughter Ellen had vanished. She had gone to the theatre as usual, performed in *The Household Fairy'* at the Queen's Theatre in Long Acre, London – after that … nothing. No warning – no message – just silence. Their other children were asleep, restlessly turning from side to side, sensitive to the anxiety that swamped their household. Nell had been such a lively fun-loving elder sister until three years ago when, at the age of sixteen, she married the famous painter George Frederick Watts, thirty years her senior, and went to live with him in Little Holland House. The children did not know what had happened when suddenly, ten months later, Nell was sent home in disgrace. Gone were her smiles, her laughter. She never seemed to come downstairs. These days she spent most of her time darning their stockings. Silent, withdrawn – just a hint of a smile when they ran to her. Now she had disappeared – no one knew where.

There was a loud banging on the front door. Grabbing his robe, Ben Terry hurried downstairs. Drawing back the bolts, he opened the door. A large burly policeman stood there.
"I'm sorry, sir. It's about your daughter Ellen. We think we have found her. I am afraid she is dead, sir. Drowned. We need you to come and identify the body."

"Drowned!" Sarah's terrified voice made Ben turn round. He put his arms round his trembling wife. They were both remembering the picture postcard of a painting by Watts that they had found in Ellen's bedroom. Two words "Found Drowned" were pinned to it. They shuddered as they thought of Watts's sad painting, depicting the dead body of a young girl found in the Thames.

8. G. F. Watts. *Found Drowned.*
Oil on canvas. ca. 1848-50

Throwing on his clothes, Ben Terry rushed out of the house, leaving his wife stunned with shock. He hurried to the mortuary with the policeman. Tears running unchecked down his cheeks, Ben Terry gazed at the dead woman before him. "That's her!" he whispered. "That's Nell! Oh, Nell, why? Why?"

He left the morgue and trudged slowly back to Kentish Town. He didn't need to say a word to Sarah. She knew as soon as she opened the door.

That day the curtains were drawn and the children dressed in black. Sarah felt bereft, distraught but somehow she knew she had to go and see the body herself. When she gazed down at the young girl, she asked the attendant to lift the skirt. She needed to see the strawberry birthmark on her left knee. She overcame her nausea and looked close – she looked at the corpse's leg and arm. There was no mark. "This is not Nell", she whispered.

"God rest her soul whoever she is, but she is not my daughter".

Hidden away in The Red House, Gustardwood Common, their love nest in the Hertfordshire countryside, Ellen Terry and her lover Edward Godwin heard the reported news of Ellen's 'death'.

ELLEN: *"I flew up to London to give ocular proof to my poor distracted parents that I was still alive. Mother, who had been the only one not to identify the drowned girl, confessed to me that she was so like me that, just for a second, she too was deceived."*

Ben and Sarah forgave Ellen, but in their hearts they recognised the truth. She was still married to Watts and was living with another man. Surely she must recognise that she was now a 'fallen woman'. She had sacrificed her career as an actress and her life in society. Her name was taboo. When Lewis Carroll came to call and asked after her, Ben and Sarah said she was staying in lodgings and only visited from time to time. They were too ashamed to tell the truth.

In the Hertfordshire countryside, Ellen was in love and deliriously happy. She had first met Edward Godwin in Bath and had been deeply attracted by the unusual simplicity of his home, for he was an architect who rejected the heavy furnishings of the Victorian era for the simplicity of Japanese décor. Godwin introduced Ellen to a house that had been carefully designed so that each article complemented the other. "*For the first time*" she wrote, "*I began to appreciate beauty, to observe, to feel the splendour of things…*" In Bath she was fourteen years old, young, lively, full of spirit and vitality. She and her sister Kate were a great success and there was always a clutch of admirers at the stage door when they left to go home, well-chaperoned by their mother. Godwin was married but his wife was ailing. He was attracted by Ellen and Kate. As a part-time theatre critic, he frequented the theatre, writing his "Jottings" for the local paper. The Terry girls were often invited to his home in Portman Square. At first Mrs Terry was hesitant about their visits to his home, but reassured by friends that there would be no breach of propriety, she gave her permission. Ellen and Kate were welcomed at Godwin's home and the spark of a lasting relationship was kindled. By the time they met again in London, Ellen was married to Watts and Godwin was a widower. Remembering the vibrant young girl he had admired in Bath, he visited her at home in Little Holland House, where Watts had his studio. Their friendship was renewed and many was the time when Ellen and Watts would walk to Baker Street and visit Godwin at his office.

One day, out on her own, Ellen called on him and found him ill with fever. Having nursed her siblings, she recognised the symptoms and giving no thought to propriety, decided to stay overnight, heating poultices and nursing him. The next morning, on her return to Little Holland House, she was confronted by her parents and her husband, who accused her of infidelity. No matter how much she protested her innocence, no one would believe her and she was sent home in disgrace.

Life became increasingly unbearable and her clandestine meetings with Godwin soon developed into the full blown love affair that prompted her to make the huge decision to abandon family, friends and the theatre and live a rural life with the man she loved. "I have the simplest faith" she wrote in her 'Memoirs', "that absolute devotion to another human being means the greatest happiness".

It was a lonely existence in the country. The Red House in which they lived was not in the village, so there were no neighbours to call on her. Her daily chores that she described so vividly meant that she was working all day long. She had animals to feed, floors to scrub and her mania for washing included her maid's hair, provoking a stern reprimand from the serving girl's mother who objected most strongly. Ellen was on her own most of the day, for Godwin left by train for London early every morning and in the evening, she would meet him in at the station in their pony and trap.

On December 9th 1869, Godwin was away when her first baby, Edith, was born, delivered by the local doctor, Dr James Quilter Rumball and his wife Elizabeth. Dr Rumball was a surgeon, a kindly man who loved music and played the violin.

He devoted most of his life to the care of the mentally handicapped, keeping a private 'lunatic asylum'. He specialised in phrenology, a pseudo-science very popular at the time and no doubt felt the bumps on the skulls of his patients, in order to interpret their various mental problems. When the good doctor's first wife Rebecca died in March 1859 aged 60, very much in need of a helpmate to assist him, he courted a spinster, Elizabeth Bocking whom he married on June 25th 1864 in Sunbury Middlesex, with his cousin, the Rev Charles Rumball officiating. He had made a wise choice. The new Mrs Rumball was a good, caring woman, who became a devoted member of Godwin's household. She recommended her niece, a Miss Bocking known as Bo, as nursemaid to Edy and later to Teddy, who was born on 16 January 1872. When her husband died, Mrs. Rumball became Ellen's housekeeper/friend. Nicknamed Boo by Edy and adored by Ellen, Mrs Rumball stayed with Ellen and her family for over thirty years.

Ellen Terry kept a notebook in which she listed the "golden days" of her life. One - when *"I first saw deep in a wood splashes of colour. Bluebells – sheets and sheets of bluebells."*

Another *"when my girl was born, the goldenest day of all"*

The scene is set.

The reminiscences begin…….

CHAPTER ONE

"The Goldenest Day of all"

MY CHILDHOOD MEMORIES

EDY   *EDITH CRAIG*
Born Dec 9th 1869 at 5 pm at Gustardwood Common (at the Red House)

EDWARD GORDON CRAIG
Was born at Stevenage on January 16th 1872.
Mother was desperately ill. The doctor went to my father and said which would he rather lived and he said "The mother".

One of my nicknames was Bally Williams as I was nearly born there.

Edy Craig
At the age of three, driving in a two-wheeled pony cart with a grey pony. I had to be lifted up and Mother used to put me sitting between her feet and my shoulders fitted in below her knees and I used to look up into the sky and think it was night because I could see stars and I noticed little trees sticking up in the hedge and used always to be looking for the next one. Of course I could not count them and I remember that it was very cold.

Since then I heard from Mother that it was the road Gustardwood Common to Wheathamstead – and Mother was going to meet my father.

1

About the same time I remember a white bulldog who used to lie in the grass with me and if I tried to get up, he would just pull me down again. He would let me pick daisies but would not allow me to stray.

My Mother lived in Gustardwood Common in 1869 and that is where I was born. I think we were also there in 1870 as I cannot find any record of Mother being anywhere else: in 1872 my brother was born probably at Pigeons Wick, Harpenden (afterwards called Fallows Green) but I don't remember anymore and think I must have been sent to stay with someone to get me out of the way.

My first remembrance of my brother was of him being wrapped up in a red shawl and put into a wheelbarrow and sent down to 'Boo' (Mrs. Rumball who was the wife of the local doctor) with a label tied on – the label stuck out under his ear and he was very fat.

My third birthday was a great day. There were fireworks; a Catherine Wheel was fastened to the door and I wondered how it could have got there. There was also a lovely bonfire of which the flames shot up and then died down.

In *The Story of My Life*, Ellen Terry tells how she and Godwin took Edy with them to Normandy where Godwin was studying the Bayeux tapestry. She and all her subsequent biographers place the location of the following anecdote in a French cathedral. Edy has a different version.

EDY   *I SAW ANGELS*

My father was working in St. Alban's Abbey. I think I must have been about three years old. Workmen were making excavations and alterations in the Abbey and my mother and father were there. I was sitting on a pile of workmen's coats. When Mother came for me, I said to her "Miss Edy seen the angels". She said they must have been choirboys but I said that they were not and that they WERE angels. Just at this moment the shrine of St. Alban was discovered. My mother said that the workman

who came and told her that the shrine had been discovered fell in a dead
faint with emotion.

It could well be that Edy's version is the true one, bearing in mind her total recall
of the incident – the workmen's coats – the discovery of the shrine of St Alban.

Today the website of the Shrine of St Alban confirms that pieces of the shrine
were discovered at exactly that time during the 19th century restoration by the
architect Gilbert Scott. We know that Edy's father, the architect Edward Godwin
was actively involved in abbey restoration.

EDY   *Old Mr. Rumball used to come up to my nursery and play to me on the*
violin while I had my tea which consisted of bread and treacle. I can
remember that I never wore shoes and stockings in those days and always
ran about barefooted. Also that I did not seem to have very much in the
way of underclothes and my top dress was a thick flannel garment in the
winter and a thin one in summer.

             My memory at this time seems to be chiefly about Teddy who I used to
cart about and try to make do things. But the only things he seemed to
care for were to eat and sleep. He seemed to take very little active part in
life for quite a number of years. I was left very much alone or was sent
to stay with people and I used to make my own amusements. Teddy on
the other hand was generally parked out on some old lady who would
take him on her knee – he was quite passive.

As children, Teddy and Edy were always on hand to meet the many celebrated
visitors who called on Ellen Terry. There was no conventional "children should
be seen but not heard" in their home, as Edy recalls:

EDY   *People often used to come to see my mother – the following I can*
remember – Justin MacCarthy (writer) – and there was a follower of
Garibaldi called Romanetti, who Boo used to bring to see her, he was just
thrilling. Also the Forbes-Robertson family – Mr. and Mrs. I was a

> *favourite of his and Teddy was a favourite of Mrs. They were all followers of John Stewart [sic] Mill and this was my first connection with W.S. (Women's Suffrage)*

John Stuart Mill (1806-1873) was a philosopher whose liberal thinking was widely respected in the 19th century. A Member of Parliament and civil servant, he was the first person to champion the cause of women's right to vote. He was a strong advocate of proportional representation, trade unions and farm cooperatives, but women's rights were his main concern.

EDY   *Mr. Forbes Robertson was very fiery and wore his hair full at the sides. Mrs. was rather grim and I was a little bit afraid of her – not so with him. Johnston the eldest who was a painter before he went on the stage. Ian was an apprentice to a sculptor and worked in metal. He used to carry me about on the back of his neck and was extremely strong. I used to follow Johnston and carry his paintbox. Eric I did not like. He used to take me out up the lane and leave me and would vanish behind the hedge and shout to me that I was lost. This I used to believe and sometimes used to sit in the road and cry and run up and down, trying to see him through the hedge. Sometimes I used to stay with them – or if Mother went away for the day, she used to leave me with them – Frances was my particular friend – she was called Franky – she became Mrs. Harrod and used to do journalistic work later on in life.*

Ellen brought her children up to be very independent. Edy was a self-sufficient little girl with a strong character whom her nursemaid described as "a piece". Teddy had good looks and charm and was adored by all, especially old ladies. This obviously influenced Edy, whose sibling resentment is apparent throughout these childhood memories.

In the Hertfordshire countryside, the sunshine of the lovers' idyll dwindled to gloom as Godwin's success as an architect fluctuated. He travelled daily to his London office at 197 Albany Street, returning at night, often bringing his designs and plans back with him. Many was the night that Ellen harnessed the pony to the trap and drove to the station to meet him. She would watch the passengers alight, her heart sinking when Godwin was not among them. Alone and sad, she would head for home. One night she was accosted by a drunken oaf who leaped on the trap. She fought him off fiercely with her whip.

When Godwin did come home, their evenings were spent pouring over the working drawings and plans and, many years later, Ellen blamed her rapidly deteriorating eyesight on the strain of copying the details by candlelight. For relaxation they would play Bach's Preludes and Fugues, Godwin playing the bass and Ellen the treble.

EDY   *Between the ages of 2 and 3, I used to hear Bach's Preludes and Fugues played to me before I went to bed. These were played by my father on the piano (he was also a very good organist) I used to choose the ones I liked best and I had names for them. My favourite one I called "Bally Williams one"; the others I knew by little drawings which my father made by the side of them and some he used to mark with a special mark thus:*

This drawing or mark meant my mother, myself and my father. This shows that I could not have been very old as my brother had no mark.

Ten years earlier in Bristol, Godwin had been friendly with an architect, Henry Crisp, an impressive young man whose strawberry spotty complexion appeared to be a family trait. It was to Crisp that Godwin turned for help whenever his poor health prevented him from travelling, and so it was no surprise when in January 1864, they decided to enter into partnership. After Godwin's successful commission to build the Northampton Town Hall, his future seemed assured. However things went badly wrong when he undertook the construction of a very large house to be built for the Hon. Roland Winn at Glenbegh, County Kerry, Ireland. The construction costs exceeded the estimate and proved a disaster when the fierce winter gales drove the rain through the walls. Crisp was forced to investigate many companies specialising in damp coursing. No one ever knew why the wet persisted – perhaps it was caused by Winn's sudden decision to add a tower and circular room. In January 1871, Godwin's partnership came to an end, hastened by a dispute over an additional £600, which Godwin had charged for extra furniture designs. By now, Godwin had used up all his own funds in order to build a house for his family, Fallows Green at Harpenden, Hertfordshire.

Fallows Green was a large house set in twenty acres of ground. Like his home in Bristol, Godwin designed an interior in his favourite Japanese style. Indeed, Ellen and Edy both dressed in kimonos, Edy's being a gift from the artist Whistler. Ellen was ecstatically happy there but she was a total disaster when it came to budgeting her household expenses. Soon it became obvious to her that her children were going to suffer, if she did not go back to work.

One famous day in the autumn of 1873, Ellen was driving through the country lanes with Edy and Teddy. Deeply worried by the threat of the bailiffs at Fallows Green, she was startled when a wheel of the trap suddenly fell off and she found herself stranded with two young children and a pony. No one was hurt and reassuring the children, she climbed out and stood in the road, wondering what to do next. She realised she was in the path of a hunt, when suddenly a crowd of horsemen leapt over the hedge, chasing a fox. One of the riders, a large, bearded gentleman spotted the poor girl and reined in his horse, calling out "Can I help you?" Then, looking hard at her, he exclaimed "Good God, it's Nelly! Where have you been all these years?"

The rider was the author and dramatist, Charles Reade. Ellen told him she was very happy, enjoying living in the country. Reade said whether she was happy or not was not relevant. It was high time she returned to the stage. "No, never" she declared.

Charles Reade did not give up so easily. He was looking for a new leading lady to play Philippa Chester in his play *The Wandering Heir*, a convoluted melodrama based on a true case of false impersonation.

"You're a fool" he told Ellen when she firmly turned down his offer. "You ought to come back".

"Suddenly" wrote Ellen later, "I remembered the bailiff in the house a few miles away and I said laughingly "Well, perhaps I would think of it if someone would give me forty pounds a week!"

"Done!" said Reade, "I'll give you that and more."

Ellen was delighted. The promise of such a high salary meant that she could redeem the furniture in Fallows Green and settle all their debts to the local tradesmen. Godwin too made no objection, aware perhaps of the long periods when he was forced to leave her alone in the country. Neither of them worried about what would happen if *The Wandering Heir* failed nor how they would pay to set up a home in London. Godwin set to work and soon found them accommodation at 20 Taviton Street, not far from Kings Cross. They moved to London.

After six weeks, in spite of Ellen's personal success, the box office take was down so Charles Reade replaced *The Wandering Heir* with another of his plays which

9. Mrs. Elizabeth Rumball (Boo)

he staged at Astley's, the home base of Sanger's Circus. This also failed, so he decided to take his company on tour. Godwin was left alone with the children at Taviton Street, feeling moody and dejected.

Edy remembers those first days in London.

EDY   *Mother went back on the stage in 1874 and our home was broken up. Teddy and I were then all over the place, staying with friends of mother's, but we were not together. We lived a lot at Boo's house and we also stayed at her house when she had let it to the Forbes Robertsons.*

When Dr. Rumball died in June 1872, Boo valiantly endeavoured to keep the home going for his patients but as Edy describes, she was none too successful!

EDY   *Boo used to go with my mother when she went on tour. Her husband the doctor had died. He had a lunatic asylum which his wife tried to keep going after he died but the lunatics all escaped and the authorities said she must give up. They were kept in a beautiful home. She kept the house where she lived called 'The Limes' Harpenden. and that was the house she used to let to the Forbes Robertsons when she went on tour.*

Ellen wrote of Boo whom she often referred to as "my aunt"

ELLEN   [On her husband's death] *"she tried to look after the lunatics herself. But she wasn't at all successful. They kept escaping and people didn't like it. This was my gain, for Boo came to look after me instead, and for the next thirty years I was her only lunatic and she my most constant companion and dear and loyal friend."*

EDY   *We came together again in 1875 and lived at 221 Camden Road next door to the Brecknock Arms where we had rooms. At this time things were rather bad as Mother had no work and we all lived on bread and milk for about six months. She had an engagement in 'Ours' during that year but was later ill and had to leave and was out for five months.*

In 1875 Teddy and I were taken to see Mother act. Bo took us. She was the niece of Boo and was really a Miss Bocking. I think she came to look after me and Teddy in 1874. Pigeons Hoo was given up in 1873 and we lived sometimes at The Limes Harpenden with Bo looking after us. Boo was looking after Mother either in London or if she was touring. She stayed and went with her everywhere until she died.

The performance we went to see was 'Masks and Faces'. Mother did not know that we were in the front. We were up in the gallery and I was thrilled. We did not know how Teddy would behave so he was given some thick slices of bread with brown sugar in between as Bo was not sure how he would behave. I liked the play very much and I hung over the edge but Teddy sat on the floor to eat his bread and sugar which he ate solemnly.

Masks and Faces was a sentimental comic melodrama set amongst 18th century acting folk. Peg Woffington was an Irish actress, who began life as a street singer. Before coming to London in 1740, her performance as Ophelia in a 1737 production of *Hamlet* had brought her immediate fame. She was the lover of David Garrick but left him in 1744.

The plot of *Masks and Faces* is based entirely on "misunderstandings, unbridled desire and remarkable innocence". Ernest Vane has fallen in love with the great actress, Peg Woffington, much to the envy of his rival, Sir Charles Pomander. Having fixed a little party for the lady, it is inevitable that Vane's innocent wife, Mabel (played by Ellen Terry) will turn up from the country at just the wrong moment.

EDY   *I remember Mrs. Bancroft, Mr. Coghlan (Charles F. Coghlan) and Mother, especially the end of the Second Act and I wondered why Mother was hiding behind a cupboard and I wondered why Mother fainted and didn't go with Peg Woffington and Ernest Vane. She looked very long and thin.*

This however was not the first time I had been to a public performance,

10. Sir Johnston Forbes Robertson

for my mother and father had taken me to Astleys to see the circus. I remember there was a clown who walked on a slack rope, who kept falling off and there was a great bang on the drum which frightened me. My mother told me years afterwards that I had said to her "This is not the kind of performance you should have brought me to" but I do not remember having said this.

I also remember going with Johnston Forbes Robertson to Sadlers Wells. He was playing the part of Cromwell in 'Henry VIII' and Phelps was playing Wolsey. He left me in the front on a wooden bench and I enjoyed the show very much. I had a pair of cotton gloves which I hated and I was stung on the finger by a wasp and I had been told not to take off my gloves. This took away a little from my enjoyment and I was glad when Forbes Robertson came for me.

Samuel Phelps the actor was a neighbour of Ellen and her children when they lived in Camden Town. He rescued the failing Sadler's Wells Theatre, giving it a new lease of life with his productions of Shakespeare plays, some of which, like *The Winter's Tale* and *Measure for Measure* had never been performed since the days of the Globe Theatre.

EDY   *Mr Phelps used to live quite near us when we lived next door to the Brecknock and when he was very ill, Mother used to send Teddy and me round with a little jelly or soup. We liked being allowed out by ourselves and used to bring her back a bunch of flowers which we had picked in people's gardens. Laburnum was a favourite as it hung over the walls. We got to know the men who ran the trams and they used to give us rides. The tram tickets in those days used to have pictures on them and one I especially remember was one with a picture of Adeline Patti* on it. Of course I used to pick them up off the floor as we got our rides through the friendship of the tram men.*

*Adeline Patti was a famous opera singer

11. Holloway Jail

EDY   *I used to think that I would like to live in Holloway Jail – that it was a beautiful castle!*

Ellen Terry was probably one of the most photographed women in the history of the theatre. She is pictured on postcards in both her acting roles as well as at home, with her dogs, with Edy – there are literally hundreds of different photographs of her. Many beautiful portraits were taken by Alexander, the Court and high society photographer of the day. Ellen kept an album of her favourites. At that time they were collected by her fans as well as used for communicating in an age when the postal service offered several deliveries a day.

EDY   *I used to love to gaze into the windows of the photographer shops. The whole window used to be filled with photographs of actors and actresses and there was generally a crowd of people gazing at them. I used to worm my way into the front of the crowd and then point out the photographs of Mother and say to the crowd "That is my Mother!"*

When we lived in Camden Town, we used to walk to one or other of the following every day. To the British Museum – the National Gallery, where my favourite picture was 'The Bloodhound' by Landseer which I used to call 'The Bloody Greyhound', – the third place was Covent Garden to see the flowers unpacked – this was the way I got my first education. Bo took us to these places.

Camden Town 221 Camden Road
The first time Teddy and I were photographed was in Camden Town – I think it was at Hilldrop Crescent – I asked if I could have my cat with me – it was my first pet – this I was allowed to do. I was also photographed on the same day in a little Japanese kimono which Whistler had given to me. Mother said "Now then, put your hand on your hip and look daggers!" Teddy was photographed in his little sailor suit and with nothing on at all as he was supposed to be so beautiful.

12. "Look Daggers!"

My little kitten had been given to me by Charles Cottet* (?) and was called Cripto Concord Syphonos Tomato. In the end, someone kicked it and it died. I was very upset when it was hurt and died. Teddy liked the kitten but he was terrified of dogs. I liked them but I did not dare to go and speak to them because Teddy was so frightened.

* Charles Cottet (1863–1925), French painter, was born at Le Puy-en-Velay and died in Paris. In the photograph of Edy in the kimono she is about 5 in 1874 which would mean that Charles Cottet who gave her the cat would only be 12 years old at that time. So could it be Charles Cottet the painter as he was only 6 years older than Edy? I can find no trace of him in England at that time.

EDY   *From the months of July to the end of October the theatres in London were mostly closed and most of the actors used to take a holiday and some go on tour. My first journey by myself was from London to Liverpool and I was about eight. (I remember this because on my seventh birthday it was forgotten and I thought the end of the world had come! Mother was ill and I sat in a darkened room with her all day. I wondered if anyone would remember that it was my birthday – but they did not!) I was put in charge of the guards and I felt very grand.*

We lived in Liverpool in Ducie Street. The maid at the lodgings was very fat and her name was Charlotte and I liked her very much. She used to wear a chenille net on the back of her hair. While I was at Liverpool, I was taken to see 'Uncle Tom's Cabin' which was on at the Argyle Theatre. I thought it was most wonderful and when Little Eva died I was very impressed with Little Eva's diamond earrings as she sat amongst the clouds with angels surrounding her with silver crowns.
After this, Teddy had to be Little Eva and I was the villain with the stock whip – and Uncle Tom – and several other parts. I adored the gruesome parts and if it was on at any of the places we were at, I used to rush round to see it. I think Bo was very fond of it also. I was always sent to bed early so I never went to any performances at night.

This was the first time I remember the Casellas as they used to come to see Mother. Mrs. and the two girls came one day when Mother had a very bad headache. I was in the back dining room (which opened into the front drawing room) crying bitterly because Bo had been angry with me. From the earliest times I have always collected pictures. The first ones I remember collecting were pictures of horses out of a Bradshaw which was hanging up in the water closet. I used to pull the leaves out and when I got a chance, I used to cut them out. On the occasion when the Casellas called, Bo had taken them away from me and I was crying because of this. They, thinking it was because Mother had a headache, said "Never mind, dear, she will be better soon". I thought that I could not explain that I was not crying because of Mother's headache at all – but I also thought that I ought to be!

Forbes Robertson used to come to see Mother – he was devoted to her. He used to look so beautiful. I remember him dressed in a blue linen shirt, loose and open at the neck with a Byronian collar, corduroy knee breeches and blue knitted stockings – like some of Walter Crane's pictures – I had been brought up on his books so thought these clothes quite ordinary.

Mother was very strict about Art. In my nursery I had Japanese prints and very early I knew the difference between the Chinese and the Japanese which lots of people muddled up. And Walter Crane picture books we were brought up on. This was very awkward because people were always bringing presents for us – but Mother used very often to destroy them. She never let us have tin tops. I had a Noah's Ark with a dove painted on the roof. We had Chinese birds – lapis and amber.

1875 and 6. I used to call Johnston Forbes Robertson "Fuf". It was about this time 1875/76 that I first remember driving in hansom cabs. They used to have straw on the floor. I also remember being told my mother was twenty-seven years old. I was in a hansom cab when I was told this and for years and years I always thought she was twenty-seven.

1875 Madame Tussauds. Teddy and I used to go very often to the exhibition of waxworks. It used to be in Baker Street then. This was when we were living in Camden Town. As most of the figures were from life, they were better than they are today. We knew them all so well. (We would go there often when Mother was at Windsor and for being photographed.) I knew exactly how long the mechanical mouse took to come in and out of the prisoner's cell. Napoleon's carriage was the thing we loved best. It was on wonderful springs and we used to jump in and out of it. We knew it was the carriage that he went to battle in and there was a writing desk that would pull out and there was a sand shaker for drying the ink. On the other side there was a little arrangement for cooking things – and a secret pocket for maps. Our history was a little 'sticky' but we knew Napoleon very well from his pictures. There were not very many people there in those days and we looked on it as a kind of playground when Mother took us first. She thought I would be awfully frightened. I was most callous and lifted up the skirt of one of the figures and said "Oh! it's

13. Walter Crane Illustration For "The Frog Prince"

only wax!" I learnt a lot about costume and, of course, those were the real ones. Mme T's was a very much smaller place than it is now. I liked all the French Revolution people, Henry VIII and his wives etc. but the ones of Queen Victoria as she was depicted did not interest me at all.

The "cooking things" included a tea caddy where Napoleon kept diamonds, which were found when the carriage was captured. The desk too had a secret drawer, which contained jewels and money. Napoleon's carriage was destroyed by fire at Madame Tussaud's in 1925.

CHAPTER TWO

My First Theatrical Experiences

In 1762 Samuel Johnson answered an urgent call for help from the writer Oliver Goldsmith.

JOHNSON *"I received one morning a message from poor Goldsmith that he was in great distress, and, as it was not in his power to come to me, begging that I would come to him as soon as possible. I sent him a guinea, and promised to come to him directly. I accordingly went as soon as I was dressed, and found that his landlady had arrested him for his rent, at which he was in a violent passion: I perceived that he had already changed my guinea, and had a bottle of Madeira and a glass before him. I put the cork into the bottle, desired he would be calm, and began to talk to him of the means by which he might be extricated. He then told me he had a novel ready for the press, which he produced to me. I looked into it and saw its merit; told the landlady I should soon return; and, having gone to a bookseller, sold it for sixty pounds. I brought Goldsmith the money, and he discharged his rent, not without rating his landlady in a high tone for having used him so ill."*

The novel which so impressed Samuel Johnson was *The Vicar of Wakefield*, which, after an unimpressive start, has stood the test of time. The only novel that Goldsmith ever wrote, the story set in 18th century England, tells of the fortunes and misfortunes of the Vicar Charles Primrose, and his wife Deborah and their six children. A dramatic turn of events takes place when Olivia, one of the good vicar's daughters, disappears and ultimately returns home, deceived, seduced and deserted by their landlord, Squire Thornhill, the villain of the piece.

This episode in the novel was adapted for the stage by Goldsmith's fellow Irishman, W.G. Wells under the title *Olivia*. When John Hare invited Ellen to join his company at the Court Theatre, he gave her what she described as "the second great opportunity of my career". With the charismatic William Terriss playing Squire Thornhill, Ellen's performance as Olivia was so moving that the audience invariably left in tears – and Ellen herself had difficulty in controlling her own emotions. No doubt her audiences were aware of Ellen's own sad circumstances as, by now, Godwin had left her and she was a single mother of two illegitimate children. She, Edy and Ted were not even welcome at Moray Lodge, the luxurious home of her sister Kate. To restore her social status, Ellen needed to find a husband. She had many suitors, among them the handsome Johnston Forbes Robertson and another the less attractive Charles Kelly Wardell.

EDY   *In 1876 Mother went to the Court Theatre and it was at this time that I knew Charles Kelly. I loved him – he was very big and strong and one day he was lying on the sofa and I used to jump up and down on him and one day I rolled him off and he broke some of his ribs. I remember thinking that I was very strong when my mother told me I had done this. I really felt secretly proud. He used to tell me stories of the Crimean War. During the time my mother was at the Court Theatre, she and Charles Kelly were married. This did not seem to me at all strange. I remember walking on in 'Olivia' with Teddy. This was our first appearance on any stage.*

Brixton 1877-78.
Then Mother went on tour after she was married to Kelly. Teddy and I were left in Brixton. Kelly was a widower who had two sisters-in-law. Their names were Fanny and Lizzie Kernan and Mother always supported them (one was a cripple) and we were put to stay with them. I don't think they were much good but Mother was sorry for them – and one was very hard working and the other was a cripple. After the

crippled one died, the other sister never said anything about it and went on taking the same allowance. They, Fan and Lizzie, had a brother called Fred who was a member of the Salvation Army. He used to come on Sunday and say prayers and sing in a very loud voice in the very small sitting room, while we could smell the roast beef – Fred had the long beard they all wore to try and look like General Booth.

Up to this time although we had been poor, we had been brought up in the midst of culture but at Brixton the people were of quite a different kind and we were allowed – much to our enjoyment – to run about like guttersnipes. We used to make mudpies in the road. We used to buy sweets of many mixed colours, stamp them on to the pavement and then eat them. We enjoyed the slackness of all this. The only person we did not like was one Willie (or Fred) who was the brother of Lizzie and Fran. I think he must have been a salvationist as he wore a cap with a peak and he used to come to pray. We had all kinds of food that we had never had – pork and beer and sausages. This we liked.

Brixton.
Mother had been told by someone about our behaviour and was horrified. As she had to be on tour and had no home, she got a nursemaid for us (to whom we paid no attention). I think she used to come by the day and her name was Emma. There was a song at that time called 'Woa Emma' and we always thought it was about her and when boys used to sing it in the road we used, she was furious.

I remember going to the Crystal Palace – the things which stand out were chiefly the approach in which there were many booths where they sold stencils for putting your name on your handkerchiefs etc. The organ I liked very much – I could not understand the palms and did not think they were real.

While Mother was on tour, she used to get us a present for every place she went to and used to bring them all back at the end of the tour. We used to look forward to this with great excitement. She brought us lots of books and always Assafrey's Toffee from Glasgow.

End of 1876, 1877 part of 1878 after Brixton – Fulham.
After Brixton we went – Charles Kelly, Mother, Boo, Bo, Teddy and myself to rooms in 22 Finborough Road off the Fulham Road. The lodgings were kept by a French woman. We had all our meals in a basement room. In this room I also had my first French lessons from our landlady. I didn't like these lessons much. Teddy and I spent most of our time in the Brompton Cemetery, picking flowers off the graves and I knew more about that cemetery than most people. We had a magnificent playground there and the vaults always reminded us of 'Romeo and Juliet' and we used to act scenes there. Mr. Kelly's first wife was buried there and we used always go and pay a solemn visit to her grave. Teddy and I had a theory – at least I think I had it and told Teddy to believe it – i.e. that all the people who were buried by the wall with their gravestones standing up against the wall, were murderers and we used to take flowers from the more important graves and put them on some of these where there were no flowers because we were sorry for them.

1877 Charles Reade lived in a house at 19 Albert Gate, Knightsbridge. I went to lunch by myself in his house. One of those little houses between the Hyde Park Hotel and the Barracks. They wanted to pull them down then, but he fought so hard that they were left standing and were still there when I last passed. (I think they were bombed by the Germans in the 1939-1945 War) They had little gardens which were bordered at the foot of Hyde Park and I used to love to stand on the bank and look over the wall and watch the fashionable people passing by in the Park. Another thing that thrilled me very much, instead of having flowers in a pot on the table, he had a pot with a white currant bush growing out of it and we picked the currents and ate them at luncheon. It seemed to me like fairyland. He was a very exciting and interesting person to be with. I don't know why I was there at all because I did not go out at that age and lived in the country. I did not come to live in London permanently *until Mother got the engagement at the Court Theatre which was a settled thing. Charles Reade had a short beard and looked more like a sea captain, his hair and beard were grey and he had a round, piercing dark eye and didn't seem to me to be very tall. C.R. was a tremendous admirer of Wilkie Collins.*

Charles Reade (1814-1884) took great care that posterity would recognize his achievements in the correct order when he left a wish that the word 'dramatist' should take first place on the list engraved on his tombstone. In spite of this he is best remembered for his novel *The Cloister and the Hearth.*

EDY   *We were very interested in the Lillybridge [sic] Sports Grounds. Someone used to take us there on Saturday afternoons. There we used to see the Royal Family, the Duke of Clarence, Duke of York, later King George V, The Princess Royal who were with their father and mother King Edward VII and Alexandra. The children used to wear sailor hats and they drove in a carriage with prancing horses. There was a cinder track and this was used for bicycle races. The bicycles had a very tall front wheel and a little one at the back. There was also running, jumping hurdles, putting the weight, throwing the hammer. There was no great crowd like there is nowadays.*

There was a dairy just off the Fulham Road and it was great excitement for us to go and see the cows milked. Much to our sorrow it was taken away and a roller skating place built on the site and now there are flats built on it.

1877 Brancaster. (Norfolk coast)
In Brancaster while staying with Bo in her cottage. Her father was a fisherman and he used to go out fishing and used to come back with crabs, lobsters, mackerel, shrimps and little fish. They used to be cooked and he used to take them in a basket or on a cart and sell them. The copper was always kept ready. In Brancaster I slept in an attic papered with newspapers (like the Wordsworth attic). It was an excitement to see

the pictures during a storm at night in the light of the lightning flashes.

The guidebook to Dove Cottage and the Wordsworth Museum in the Lake District confirms that Wordsworth's sister Dorothy papered the children's bedroom with newspapers to keep out the draughts.

THE COURT THEATRE *OLIVIA* 1878

EDY   *I did not come to live in London permanently until Mother got the engagement at the Court Theatre which was a settled thing.*

Mother was still at the Court and about this time they did 'Olivia' which was a bigger and better production as they found Mother could play the part and she made an instantaneous and very big success. We then moved to 33 Longridge Road and got more and more respectable. It was when we lived here that I first went into a dressing room.
The first dressing room I went into was that of Mrs. Banman Palmer. Nothing she did escaped me. I watched everything she did for I was spellbound with interest. Mrs. BP said she was afraid of the child with the dark and piercing eyes who sat in the corner. Of course the 'make-up' was dry as there were no greasepaints in those days.

The moment I saw two people talking together about the theatre I used to immediately attach myself to them to listen. When I was interested I used to stare so hard at people that when they didn't know me, they used to wonder what was the matter. But I was very privileged in the theatre and people were awfully nice to me.

There were tremendous excitements during the run of 'Olivia'. I went to a rehearsal for the first time. John Hare was producing the play and William Terriss was in the play. He was a great favourite with Teddy and me. He used to egg me on. On one occasion he was running after me. I took a short cut, ran into a beautiful gate-legged antique table and knocked down a piece of scenery that was not properly fixed. I managed to get under the table which scared me (as I was quite small) but the table was smashed and Mother was covered with confusion and I had to apologise to Mr. Hare of whom I was terrified. Terriss took all the blame but Mother was very angry with me and I was always very well behaved at rehearsal after this.

'Olivia' ran for some time. This was the first time that Teddy and I walked on, in the first act. It must have been in the summer as I remember that Teddy and I brought bunches of real flowers from the country and gave them to Mother.

Since then I played Polly Flamborough, the gypsy and Sophie in that play. It was only for one matinée that Teddy and I walked on. We were always sent to bed about 6 pm. No late hours. Teddy's cheeks were so red that they made the makeup on the other actors look pale.

During the run of 'Olivia', the little girls who played the children in 'Olivia' were brought to have tea with us. I hated them because they had blue silk dresses. I wanted one and Mother always dressed me in cotton dresses from Liberty's and pinafores which I had to make myself. I remember being very proud that the cap that Mother used to wear in 'Olivia' being copied in all the shop windows as it became the fashion and was called the "Olivia bonnet". This made me feel very proud.

I think it was from this time on that I began to know people on the stage – actors such as John Hare, William Terriss, Hermann Vezin. I always adored the comedians Anson, I also liked Cathcart and I liked the older women Mrs Gaston Murray. It seems to me now that I always liked the ones who could really do something as I don't remember the others at all.

Ellen's popularity was now nationwide. There were *Olivia* bonnets, *Olivia* postcards and photographs. However, Charles Kelly, Ellen's husband was not happy. Peeved and jealous, he had only been offered a minor part which he refused, declaring he wanted the role of the Vicar, Olivia's father. He was drinking heavily. In an attempt to appease him, Ellen organised a tour with him where their performances were well received in the provinces. But basically Kelly was an alcoholic and gradually their relationship deteriorated until it failed and they separated.

Just before *Olivia* closed, Ellen received a letter that would change her life once again. It was dated July 20, 1878 and it came from 15a Grafton Street.

"*Dear Miss Terry, I look forward to the pleasure of calling upon you on Tuesday next at two o'clock. With every good wish, believe me, yours sincerely – HENRY IRVING*".

It was a very awkward meeting. Ellen thought she knew what he was going to offer her but nothing was certain. Irving was quiet and gentle. They both felt ill at ease, uncomfortable. She could not understand why he was being so vague about his proposition. He told her he had leased the Lyceum and was going to manage it. Irving actually believed he had made it clear that he was engaging her to be his leading lady at the Lyceum, but in truth, he was quite vague and offered her no firm proposal. Ellen was not accustomed to such a formal stiff atmosphere. Suddenly both of them turned at the same time to see Irving's dog Charlie squat and make a mess on the carpet. There was confusion. Irving apologising for his dog, Ellen reassuring him that she was a dog-lover and understood. They both rushed to the fireplace and grabbed the fire tongs and the hearth brush. Ellen began to giggle as they tried to clear up the mess and they both ended up laughing so much that the ice was broken and the friendship forged.

Edy and Ted were obviously not about at the time of the meeting as Edy makes only one reference to that all-important day.

EDY   *While we were at Longridge Road, Henry Irving came to see Mother and engaged her to play Ophelia at the Lyceum.*
        I don't remember the first night of 'Ophelia'. I think we were probably sent down to the country while Mother was studying her part and she was far too tactful to let her children come playing about the theatre.

The first night of *Hamlet* at the Lyceum with Irving as Hamlet and Ellen Terry as Ophelia took place on December 30th 1878. It was Irving's first production and he had spent hours designing alterations to the theatre, putting in new seats and a new drop curtain. He rehearsed all the actors over and over again – all, that is, except Ophelia. Ellen became increasingly nervous as the first night grew nearer and eventually plucked up courage to ask him "Couldn't we rehearse our scenes?" "WE shall be alright" he answered tersely. So, on the first night, as soon as Ophelia died, Ellen hurried out of the theatre, and spent the next hours driving up and down the Embankment, staring at the river, convinced that she had failed miserably. She was not there to take her bow when the curtain came down. She did not see the flowers thrown on the stage. Irving took all the curtain calls. He was delighted. His new leading lady had enchanted the audience. He bowed and made a curtain speech. At home Ellen went to bed, dejected and totally convinced she was a failure.

Next day the rave reviews of her "exquisite" performance reassured her and set her firmly on the road to international acclaim.

CHAPTER THREE
Schooldays And Holidays

EDY   *Kensington. When we went to live at Longridge Road in 1878, we went to a day school. I don't know why we went there – whether it was recommended to Mother or just because it was in the next road. I expect it was because the Sickerts were there. Walter Sickert was in the cast of 'Hamlet'. He called himself Mr. Nemo in the cast. His two brothers were at this school. The school was in Topster Road and kept by a Mrs. Cole and I never had any schooling except from this family.*

Teddy and I liked it. We were very backward – we had never learnt any school book psychology. It made it very interesting that Mr.Sonnenshine [sic] who wrote the arithmetic book* should visit the school being a friend of Mrs.Cole's. I liked him because he did not mind how I got my answers to the sums provided that they were right. I had my own patent way of getting there and the governesses used to ask me how I did it and if it was not the usual way, they used to be cross – but Mr. S. didn't mind.

* 'The Science and Art of Arithmetic' by Adolf Sonnenschein and H.A. Nesbitt

1880
During the run of 'Hamlet' – the oldest Sickert (Walter) under the name of Mr. Nemo walked on and Arthur Pinero also acted a small part and two little girls of the theatre, the daughters of Mother's dresser (Flo and May Holland) were great friends of ours. They were both pages.

Mr. Nemo
It is worth mentioning that the painter Walter Sickert is now listed as a suspect

in the notorious Jack the Ripper serial murders in the Whitechapel area of London in 1888. The American crime novelist/forensic scientist, Patricia Cornwell, firmly believes that Walter Sickert was Jack the Ripper. Some of the letters of Jack the Ripper were signed 'Mr Nemo' but this phrase was in common use at the time, having the same connotation as 'Anonymous'. Ms. Cornwell even went to the extent of destroying some of Walter Sickert's paintings to try to prove her theory by matching Sickert's DNA with that of the Ripper. She also pointed out that the expressions "ha ha", a phrase frequently found in the Ripper's letters, is a "peculiarly American laugh". In her book published in 2002 *Portrait of a Killer, Jack the Ripper – Case Closed,* she suggests that Walter Sickert was imitating the annoying laugh of his friend James Whistler, the American artist. She did not prove her case and the mystery of the Ripper's true identity remains unsolved.

Edy of course had no knowledge of this but the following anecdote does imply that even as children, the Sickerts had a questionable choice of childhood games.

EDY   *At this school there were two sons of Edwin Arnold the poet and they were particular friends of ours. One was Gilbert Arnold and the other William. There was also Walter Raleigh. He was bigger, taller and knew more than we did and we liked him but with a certain respect.*

The Sickerts, the Arnolds, Teddy and myself formed ourselves into a band of terrorists and we used to have meetings at street corners with concealed daggers and on one occasion we broke a street lamp, but I think there was more plotting than actual doing.

We used to have the school desk that is now in the museum at the farm – in the basement room in Longridge Road. It faced the window and the other children used to come and look down and shake the railings and shout to us. I used to have the right hand desk and Teddy the left. Teddy and I got on very well but he was considered slow. We were both miles above the others in literature, drawing and painting, music etc but did not know ordinary schoolbook stuff.

HOLIDAYS

Boulogne – The Alfred Thompsons had a home there. He used to design costumes and we used to play with his children.

1879 We used to go to Boulogne for holidays with Mother. I think this used to happen in Holy Week. I hated the boat but Mother always liked it and expected us to be hearty. All I remember was that I was miserable but liked it when I got there. The thing that fascinated and also frightened me was the smell and the fair was lovely. Mother used to buy plain white china, very cheap and very good. This she could not get in England. I used to buy chipped potatoes with a little screw of salt. We used to stay at a little hotel on the front. The Casino gardens we used to play in all day long. Mother bought me a dress while we were there. It is the first dress that I can remember liking. It was called a fishwife dress. It was modelled on the lines of the fishwives. This became the fashion. It was a sort of cerise cloth or flannel with a different underskirt.

In '79, Teddy and I were sent to Brighton with Bo where we had our photographs taken. Teddy had his hair cut very short which pleased him very much but he looked awful. I had two wisps of short hair cut like a boy. I always had it short and also looked awful. These photographs were to be a great surprise for Mother. They were collected and put into a locket. It was an Indian locket. At this time Mother was playing a part called 'Butterfly' which was in a play translated 'Froufrou' and in it when she was dying she asks for a locket with the portrait of her children. This honour was sprung upon her and she saw these appalling looking children. I think it says much for her powers as an actress that she got through the rest of the scene. This locket with the two photographs is at Smallhythe. Teddy looking like a prize fighter and me like a guttersnipe. It happened in Glasgow Sept 1879.

14. Fred Terry, Ellen's younger brother

EDY   *Then I very much remember the first appearance of Uncle Fred – this*
was in the Crystal Palace,(?) 'New Men and Old Acres' he played the
part of Bertie FitzWise. Uncle Fred seemed to us to be of our own class
and used to play with us, but of course he was older and used to be a bit
patronising sometimes, patting us on the head. He used to play the banjo.
I remember him standing at the side waiting to go on – he was shaking
so much with nervousness that a pile of books which he was carrying kept
falling down and Mother kept picking them up and picking them up
again.

About this time Pinero became a very great favourite of mine. He was so nice to me and I admired him very much and thought he was very nice.

Sir Arthur Wing Pinero (1855-1934) English dramatist was born in London, the son of a Sephardic Jewish solicitor. He studied law at Birkbeck Literary and Scientific Institution before going on the stage. Pinero joined the Lyceum Theatre company in London in 1876 and began writing plays shortly afterwards, and became one of the most prolific and successful playwrights of his time.

EDY   *Sometimes I used to go on tour and be sent back after a bit and sometimes I used to go on tour for the latter part of the tour – Charles Brookfield and Norman Forbes were the two people I remember best in the Company. They were always up to practical jokes and behaved very badly. At Leamington they dressed up as old invalids and were wheeled to the theatre in bathchairs and, on a night when they were not playing, they came to see the rest of the company, dressed thus and pretending they were deaf, shouted remarks to each other. I was always looking out for what they would dress up as next.*

Teenage School arrangements aged 14-16

1883 Mother went on her first tour to America and I became a boarder at Mrs. Cole's school in Victoria Road where I had formerly been a day girl and Teddy was already at a boarding school – I think it was somewhere in Mayfield in Kent. Edy Gordin,(?) Cody Black (?) and myself used to go about together but I didn't make many friends in school.

1885 – until October 1886 – I went to Dixton Manor Gloucester. Here I had the best time when I was young. Mrs. Cole with whom I had been in school in London had five sisters all of whom were exceptional women, more like women of today. They were all suffragists and it was to Mrs. Malleson (I think it was the eldest sister) that I now went. I was much too difficult at school and upset the other girls and Mrs. Cole who was very fond of me, sent me to her sisters. I always liked being with older people. Mrs. Malleson had three daughters all of whom had been either at Newham or Girton, one who had taken her degree in history (she was Mabel) and used to teach me constitutional history which I hated and could never understand.

Mrs. Malleson herself taught me English literature out in the garden under the trees – we both loved Dickens and used to roar with laughter and this was my literature lesson – and she also taught me physiology and we cut up a cow's eye to see how it was made. I loved this.

The household consisted of Mrs. Malleson, who ran the farm, a cowman called Lane, a coachman called Haynes and a French woman called Azellia who did most of the work. She had boots covered with mud, her khaki skirt and a respectable outer skirt which she used to turn up and a huge apron over all this. They lived in a little dank cottage. In one half she lived with her sister Caroline and she taught me French. Caroline was quite odd. The custom was very much divided between getting the lunch ready and she used to have to rush out when she heard anything frizzle. She was a scream. She must have been about 50 years old. She was very much a lady and wore earrings and was a great friend of the clergyman's wife, who lived quite a long way off and I used to have to go with her. On other Sundays I went to church at Winchcomb. The Mallesons were all Unitarians but I used to be sent to Church as they thought I ought to go.

Mrs. Malleson was a Whitehead and her old mother who was about 90 used to live with them. She wore her hair in clusters of white curls kept together with a band of black velvet.

EDY'S FIRST EXPERIENCES OF WOMEN'S SUFFRAGE.

At that time the Women's Suffrage movements was divided into two distinct groups. The Women's Social and Political Union (W.S.P.U.) was a splinter group led by Emmeline Pankhurst and her two daughters, Christabel and Sylvia. They were known as 'suffragettes' and had no qualms about using violent, often illegal tactics to further their aims for equality for women and their demonstrations often ended in total disorder.

The other group was the original society, National Union of Women's Suffrage Societies. (N.U.W.S.S.) founded in 1897. They were led by Millicent Fawcett, the sister of Elizabeth Garrett Anderson, the first woman to gain a medical qualification in Britain who created a medical school for women. Unlike the Pankhursts, Mrs Fawcett preferred a more moderate approach. Her husband was a politician and Mrs Fawcett's aim was to change public opinion. Her followers welcomed men into their society and tried to reach their goal by reasoned argument as opposed to the violent demonstrations and hunger strikes of the suffragettes. Mrs Fawcett's followers were known as 'suffragists".

EDY   *There was great excitement when Mrs. Malleson (who belonged to Mrs. Fawcett's lot) went on a deputation to the Houses of Parliament re women's suffrage. I think she used to go up to London to suffrage meetings. This is the first time that it was explained to me.*

One daughter, Janet, taught me music, piano and theory. The daughters were not always at home but when they were they used to teach me. I don't think Alice taught me anything. She used to be away a lot and was rather spoken about with bated breath. She was under the "awful" influence of a "Roman" [sic] catholic and became one afterwards. I wondered why there was such a fuss and when I heard she had been to Rome, I thought "Oh! how nice!" She used to play duets with me when she was staying there.

If Mabel had only given me 'Green's Illustrated History', I should have learnt it from cover to cover and loved it. But I had to learn it from a nasty cheap little edition with no pictures, so hated it.

I used to go to special lessons in music to Cheltenham College. I used to go in a little pony cart by myself and when I was by myself I used to sit in the shaft like the carters – the pony didn't like this at all. Later I used to go on a bicycle which Mother gave. I belonged to the first ladies' bicycling club at Hammersmith of which Mother was the President. I remember [when] my bicycle was given to me. [It] was delivered at the Lyceum Theatre and I rode all the way from the theatre at night to Kensington without a lamp.

In the holidays I used to go up to London and stay with Mother. When I was at the Mallesons, I used to ride all over the county and I used to go to Broadway where lived Edwin Abbey, Alfred Parsons, Milletts, Pembertons (who wrote 'Ellen Terry and her Sisters', which the sisters didn't like) – and Maude Valérie White – I knew them all in London.

Edwin Austin Abbey 1852-1911 illustrator
Alfred Parsons 1847-1920 Landscape painter
T. Edgar Pemberton writer of *Ellen Terry and her Sisters*
Maude Valérie White 1855-1937 French-born Composer

EDY   *I remember bicycling over on a very hot day and going to the Abbey's and going straight into the garden. I didn't see Abbey, he was drawing a picture and I walked right into it. The people were all in 18th century clothes but it looked lovely and just right. Frank (Frederick) Barnard's two girls and Sargent used to go there a lot. And the picture 'Carnation, Lily, Lily, Rose' was painted in that garden by Sargent.*

15. Carnation, Lily, Lily, Rose 1885-6
by John Singer Sargent

It is in the Tate. These two girls and myself used to have great games. In the stables there was a hearse and we used to climb in and out of it. It had black feathers at the corners. Broadway was a beautiful place, but just an ordinary village. Now it is a show place and if a daisy comes up on the green verge, everyone goes out to pull it out and Americans pay huge money to stay at the Inn which is all Tudor. It is a very beautiful Tudor village.

CHAPTER FOUR

GROWING UP

16. Sadness – Ellen Terry 1864
Photo by Julia Margaret Cameron

Ellen Terry had known the Poet Laureate, Alfred Tennyson for many years. In 1862 the painter G.F. Watts invited Kate Terry to pose for him and Ellen was sent to accompany her. The cantankerous artist decided to paint them both and subsequently became enamoured of the exquisite younger sister. Ellen Terry became his child-bride aged 16 and went to live at Holland House. Ellen explained that Little Holland House, where Mr Watts lived, seemed to her "a paradise where only beautiful things were allowed to come. All the women were graceful and all the men were gifted." The household was run by three of the seven Pattle sisters, a demanding trio consisting of Mrs Alice Prinsep, Lady Somers, and Mrs Julia Cameron (the pioneer photographer) who were known as Beauty, Dash and Talent. They revelled in their 'court' at Little Holland House where Gladstone, Disraeli and Browning were among Mr Watt's famous visitors. These demanding women controlled G.F. Watts and treated his young bride as an ignorant nonentity. Ellen's dreams of an artistic paradise were shattered. When she went on honeymoon to the Isle of Wight, they all accompanied the bride and groom, staying in Dimbola, the home of Julia Cameron. Tennyson was a near neighbour at Farringford.

Early one morning Julia Cameron woke Ellen and took her, still in her chemise, over to Tennyson's where she took the famous portrait of her in Tennyson's bathroom. Ellen wrote:

ELLEN *At Freshwater I first saw Tennyson.*
Tennyson was more to me than a magic-lantern shape, flitting across the blank of my young experience, never to return.

The first time I saw him he was sitting at the table in his library and Mrs. Tennyson, her very slender hands hidden by thick gloves, was standing on a step-ladder handing him down some heavy books. She was very frail, and looked like a faint tea-rose. After that one time I only remember her lying on a sofa.

In the evening I went walking with Tennyson over the fields, and he would point out to me the differences in the flight of different birds. He taught me to recognise the barks of trees and to call wild flowers by their names. He picked me the first bit of pimpernel I ever noticed. Always I was quite at ease with him. At Freshwater I was still so young that I preferred playing Indians and Knights of the Round Table with Tennyson's sons, Hallam and Lionel, and the young Camerons, to sitting indoors noticing what the poet did and said. I was mighty proud when

I learnt how to prepare his daily pipe for him. It was a long churchwarden and he liked the stem to be steeped in a solution of sal volatile or something of that kind, so that it did not stick to his lips. But he and all the others seemed to me to be very old.

One charming domestic arrangement at Freshwater was the serving of the dessert in a separate room from the rest of the dinner. And such a dessert it always was – fruit piled high on great dishes in Veronese fashion, not the few nuts and an orange of some English households.

It must have been some years after the Freshwater days, yet before the production of 'The Cup' that I saw Tennyson in his carriage outside a jeweller's shop in Bond Street.
"How very nice you look in the daytime" he said. "Not like an actress".

17. "Tennyson reading"
by Helen Allingham

> *I disclaimed my singularity and said I thought actresses looked very nice in the daytime!*

Remembering her own childhood days at Freshwater, it was therefore perfectly natural that Ellen Terry would take Edy with her to the home of the Poet Laureate to hear him read *The Cup*.

EDY
> *1880* aged 11
>
> *I remember going with Mother (dressed up in my best clothes) to see the Poet Laureate, Alfred Tennyson who Mother knew well – it was to read his play 'The Cup' which he read himself to Henry Irving, Mother, William Terriss, Lady Tennyson and others present. I wasn't a bit afraid of him but Mother was rather afraid of what I should say or do. I didn't like his reading of the play and I could see that Henry Irving didn't and was dying for him to get the play and read it himself in his home – also Terriss didn't understand a word of it. I was supposed to be quite quiet but when Tennyson had finished the first scene, he turned to the company and said "Is that quite clear? The two names Synorix and Sinnatus being rather alike?" There was a rumble of conversation as no one liked to say what they really thought (no one being at all clear). I came out with a loud "No" and Tennyson couldn't believe his ears and I was hushed. I liked 'The Cup' as a play very much because there were two lovely staghounds in it. One was called Jack and he became our own dog afterwards. They used to dash across the stage in the first scene.*
>
> *Although I was behind the scene I never lost the illusion – and I was very shocked with Mother who told some people who were not on the stage, that that there was a man with a large piece of beef steak in the wings at the other side of the stage which made them strain at the leash.*
>
> *When Jack was our dog he used to bound along by my mother's carriage, sometimes along the Strand, he ran on the pavement and sometimes when she was driving in Richmond Park. She always liked to have a dog but could not give them much exercise so they always used to run behind*

her carriage. The kind she normally had were smooth-hair fox terriers but Henry gave her this one after the play.

'The Cup' was not a long enough play to fill the bill so 'The Corsican Brothers' used to be acted after it. This, at this time, was my favourite play – I always used to go to the matinées and I was allowed to walk on in the ballroom scene with a domino mask on.

In the ballroom scene there was not much action and friends of ET, who were in the audience who came round in the interval were given a domino mask and used to go and sit in the boxes on the stage (the stage was set as the Paris Opera House) and this was how I got on. After the act the people went back to their places in their part of the house.

In this scene they had a most wonderful crystal chandelier – this chandelier had been used in the auditorium, but when electric light came in, it was taken on to the stage. I can remember at a revival of 'The Corsican Brothers' just after a performance, it fell and the stage was a mass of broken crystal. If it had happened when the stage was full, a lot of people might have been badly hurt or killed. I still have a suitcase full of some of the crystal.

I remember John Barker's shop (which was a little two-countered shop in those days) because there was a boy who used to stand outside, giving away advertising leaflets which I used to collect. In fact I used to take them whenever they were offered to me and thought I should love to be one of the people who gave them away. In the end I had collected quite a pile and supplemented this by some leaves of advertisement out of our old Bradshaw which hung by a string in a 'certain place'. One day Teddy and I went up and down the Longridge Road giving them to all the people who passed by. Mother was having a tea-party on this particular day and several of the guests arrived with the paper still in their hands. One of the guests told Mother who afterward suggested to us that we should play some other game.

1880 In this year Mother took a cottage "Myrtle Cottage" at Hampton Court where Mother went for a rest to keep herself fit for her work. It was a tiny little cottage (it is now a tearoom). It is in a row and was next to Rose Cottage. Of course there was no such thing there as any teashops in those days. The only shop was an Italian shop where you could get lemonade, which was in the same row of cottages and exactly opposite the Lion Gates. We were nearer the green; the backs of these houses have no gardens and Bushey Park came up to the back windows and when we were staying there we used to feed the deer from the back windows and sometimes if we put anything on the windowsill to cool, they used to come and take it.

The men who looked after the gates and grounds were old pensioners who had been to the Crimean War. They became our greatest friends. Our favourite one had bulging eyes and a purple face and had one arm off – he was supposed to be very terrifying but we had no fear of him and liked him very much.

In the evening after the gates were shut, we used to give a performance to these men in a place that was called the Wilderness, which was a tangle of trees and shrubs between the Lion Gate and the formal gardens of the Palace. Teddy and I used to be preparing all day for the performance. The play which seemed to us to be most suitable was 'As You Like It'. This was the only play in which I allowed Teddy to play the hero. I generally took that part myself but in this play he was allowed to play Orlando. He knew most of the words of the first scene and we used to play different parts in other scenes. The pensioners used to pat us on the back and appeared to be very pleased with these performances.

The Maize [sic]. There was a platform where one of the pensioners used to direct people who lost themselves. We very soon learnt all his patter and we used to get up on to the platform and direct the people.

We used to name all the trees in the Wilderness different names. One lovely tree on a perfectly round piece of grass we christened 'Robinson Crusoe' – another, a silver birch we named 'Iolanthe' because we thought it looked like Mother in that part – another we called 'Portia' and 'Ophelia'.

In the Spring, there is a certain birdsong that whenever I hear it even now, I imagine myself back, lying on the grass under the shade of 'Iolanthe'.

1880 I went on tour with Mother and we went to Winlaton, near Newcastle on Tyne where Charles Kelly's father was the vicar and we stayed for that week at the vicarage. I think when they, CK and Mother went on, I was left at the vicarage. It was the first time I had ever been in a mining village and all the cottages were so different from anything I had ever seen. I used to go into all the cottages and one of the things that impressed me was to see the miners in a wooden tub. Their wives used to scrub them and turn them from black into white. Sometimes on hot days this performance used to take place in the garden.

There was a beautiful flower garden at the vicarage. I used to pick large bunches (as I have never been able to keep my hands off flowers) and take them as presents to the miners' cottages. I generally used to manage to take the bouquets of flowers about teatime and got the most lovely griddle cakes, split and buttered, but the tea I could not manage. It was thick and black and the pot lived on the hob all the time. I knew what strong tea was because Mother liked it and I hated it.

My language was very Shakespearian in those days and I said to my Mother of the gardens at the vicarage "Grandpapa's clowns do not like me picking the flowers".

When Mother wanted me to be good when I was very young, she used to put me in a field and say "Miss Edy pick all the buttercups" and I immediately used to try to do this. I used always to call myself "Miss Edy".

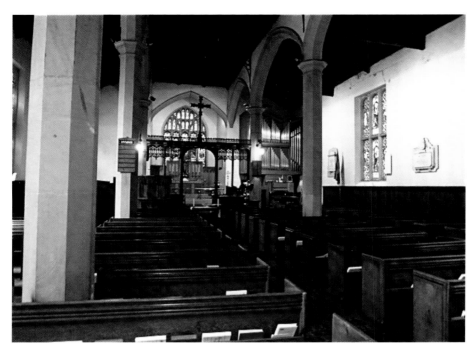

18. Interior St Paul's Church, Winlaton

> *While I was at the vicarage Mother was very particular that I should go to early service every day. Grandpapa used to get up early every morning and ring the bell and the cook-housekeeper and I used to be the congregation.*

EDY   *1880 I learnt to read at night by the light of a street lamp which shone in at my window, as the light in my room was turned off. The book was called 'That Lass O'Lowrie's' – it was all about miners.*

Published in 1878, *That Lass O'Lowrie's* was the first novel by Frances Hodgson Burnett, the author of *The Secret Garden* and *Little Lord Fauntleroy*, who later became a friend of Ellen and Edy and used to visit them at Smallhythe.

EDY   *I was taught by ear to say poems and things of Shakespeare's, then knowing the words I used to get the book and read them. I never learnt my alphabets. Directly I could read at all, I read anything I could get hold of. Some people used to say to Mother "Why do you let that child read that book?" but Mother said "Why shouldn't she? The things that are not meant for a child she will not understand." But I was always encouraged to read Scott. I think 'Ivanhoe' was one of my favourites. I liked illustrated books like 'Doré's Illustrated Bible', 'Paradise Lost', and 'Don Quixote'. These were thought suitable for Sunday and Teddy and I were very keen on them.*

Our weekday, picture books being Caldecott – Cliff books, 'Lamb's Tales from Shakespeare', 'Alice in Wonderland' and 'Through the Looking Glass', Mrs. Ewing's 'Jackanapes', 'Anderson's Fairy Tales', 'Robinson Crusoe', 'Gulliver's Travels' etc. I have got most of these books still.

My complete set of Scott were the first set of books I possessed. They were in a leather case and were given to me by Mother. Then Sir Henry Irving gave me Maria Edgeworth's* novels in calf bindings about 12 or 14 volumes.

*Maria Edgeworth (1767-1849) was an Anglo-Irish novelist.

EDY   *I had rather a mixed taste – I used to perhaps be reading some little baby's book in the morning with great enjoyment and in the afternoon 'Ivanhoe' with equal enjoyment. Just as my artistic taste varied, as I thought that a pink satin dress was beautiful – also that a Chinese print was beautiful. I loved Charles Dickens's books but Thackeray I didn't care for. I think I began wrongly on his books as 'The Yellowplush Papers' were my first and I could not understand it. I think my love of Dickens was from Newcastle, as my Grandpapa and the whole family used to rush out and buy the stories, which used to come out in parts and everyone used to be eager for them as they were all very keen. Mother knew both Dickens and Thackeray – Dickens before I was born – and Thackeray's sister used to come to see Mother at Harpenden. I used to know where he lived in Kensington Gate. I always knew whose houses we were passing when we were out walking and used to hope that the people would come out and that we should see them – but they never did. I liked to see people that I knew about.*

We used to go for walks in Kensington Gardens. How I loathed the long walk and much preferred to play on the steps of the Albert Memorial. Teddy and I had a game of how many people we could recognise on the frieze round the base of the Albert Memorial. I think the frieze on the steps of the Albert Memorial was all that we knew as we never looked higher! We had to go along Cromwell Road and up Queen's Gate to get there – how I hated this – it was the monotony that I hated. I cannot bear those thoroughfares even today.

There was a shortcut to the High Street called Wright's Lane from Cromwell Road to Barkers and it led passed the cripples' home. We always used to watch this building and hope that we should see a cripple – but we never did. The shops in Kensington High Street were all little shops in those days. Of course Earls Court was not built up and there were lots of market gardens and fields and waste patches.

Marie Corelli also lived in Longridge Road and lived with her half brother, who also wrote. We didn't like her because she didn't wear the right clothes. She used to wear a tweed suit with a pink chiffon bow put on with a safety pin. We did not think this at all right!

Marie Corelli was the 'Barbara Cartland' of her time. Her books were published in millions. She moved to Stratford-on-Avon where she lived for many years with her life long companion Bertha Vyver. She belonged to a genre of eccentric women writers. Like Edith Sitwell, she dressed strangely and attracted a lot of attention by her odd behaviour and lifestyle. She imported her own private gondola from Venice, complete with gondolier and caused quite a stir each time she went out on the River Avon.

Later on of course, Edy's own lifestyle with Christopher St John also caused many a raised eyebrow! It is obvious from her remarks that even as a child, Edy was very aware of clothes, costumes and the 'correct mode of dress', something that became an integral part of her expertise in costume design for the stage.

19. Marie Corelli in her own private gondola complete with gondolier on the River Avon.

CHAPTER FIVE

Clothes and Costumes

From early childhood Edith Craig was interested in clothes and costumes. Witnessing the success of her mother as Portia, followed by Olivia and Ophelia, she became aware of the importance of Ellen's stage costumes and their historical significance. As a child, she watched from the wings, witnessing the entrances and exits of such great actors as Henry Irving and William Terriss and gradually she became more and more intrigued with the design and making of their costumes. At that time, no expense was spared to reproduce the elaborate costumes called for in the historical plays of Shakespeare.

Later Edy would design and make costumes out of remnants and scraps and, depending on the resources of the clients for whom she was working, re-making existing garments with amazing dexterity, using old bodices and scraps of lace and ribbons that she had carefully saved for the purpose. Her scrap bag was legendary and she could work wonders with a few scarves. It is interesting to note how, as she recalls many of the personalities in these memoirs, she nearly always describes the kind of clothes they wore.

Edy also learnt from great masters of the art of costume design, first and foremost among them her own father, Edward Godwin. In 1875 he was commissioned to do the design for the production of *The Merchant of Venice* for Squire and Mrs. Bancroft, when Ellen would play Portia. Godwin went to Italy, imported genuine materials and the visual success of the play was instant. Sadly, in spite of Ellen's superb performance as Portia, the production was not a success due to the lacklustre acting of Charles Coghlan as Shylock. The costs outweighed the box office and the play was withdrawn.

46

EDY   *Mother had a dress we loved. The stuff came from Liberty's — it was yellow and blue speckled and we used to call it her 'froggie' dress. Mother used to wear her dresses all in one and reaching right to the ground. In our earliest days Teddy and I used to design costumes for the stage.*

Ellen was wearing the 'froggie' dress on that all important day in 1875 when Mrs. Bancroft came to call to offer Ellen the part of Portia in the Bancroft's production of *The Merchant of Venice* at the Prince of Wales Theatre. The room was empty as the bailiffs had been in and removed all the furniture, and all that remained was some Japanese matting and a cast of the Venus de Milo.

ELLEN   *"May I come in?"*
              Mrs Bancroft's wonderful grey eyes examined it curiously. The room, the statue and I myself must all have seemed very strange to her. I wore a dress of some deep yellow woollen material which my little daughter used to call the "frog dress" because it was speckled with brown like a frog's skin. It was cut like a Viollet-le-Duc tabard and had not a trace of the fashion of the time."

Godwin's love of Japanese art and design influenced Ellen's taste in clothes. In the country she wore kimonos and dresses with a very simple uncluttered line. By the time she moved to London, fashion trends were beginning to change. The bustles and unhealthy corsets of the Victorian era were soon replaced by the simple elegant lines of the Aesthetic era, featuring clothes far more comfortable to wear. These became the vogue of the elegant society ladies of London who bought most of the fabrics for their gowns from Liberty's. Arthur Liberty strongly favoured oriental styles and materials and it was there that Ellen Terry chose fabrics for herself, as well as simple plain dresses for Edy. Ellen was always ahead of her time and so it was not surprising that her children were dressed differently from their peers, which caused Edy some embarrassment.

20. Teddy, Ellen and Edy 1886

EDY   *This was the time that the aesthetic craze was on so Teddy and I suffered
in consequence. Teddy used to go to parties in a little white piqué suit
and I used to wear white Liberty silk made very plain. Teddy looked
perfectly lovely in his but hated it because all the other boys used to wear
tight Eton suits. The other children used to laugh at us which Teddy
hated more than I did, but he was a tremendous success with the old
ladies and girls which pleased him very much.*

Mother now being a great success at the Lyceum, we were allowed to

*make friends with our cousins the Lewis's who lived in Moray Lodge,
which was at the top of Campden Hill. In those days they had a paddock,
cows, ducks, chickens and turkeys and a large garden and tennis court.
(A block of flats is now built on the site – it came down to Holland
Lane). We used to go to a dancing class which was held at their home
and lots of children of the friends of Aunt Kate used to go there each
week. I was awfully envious of my cousins' clothes, particularly a dress
one of them had made of pink satin and honey-combed all over – rather
like the inside of a jewel box – but I thought it was lovely.*

Edy was obviously a skilled little needlewoman at the age of nine. We know that
at that time she used to make her own pinafores to wear over her Liberty dresses.
It is not surprising that these skills became very useful as she developed her
lifelong interest in costume design, which began at the Wardrobe at the Lyceum
theatre.

EDY   *I used to love to go up into the wardrobe and see the people working
there. Mrs. Reid was the wardrobe mistress and I thought she was
marvellous – she had a little room with a cooking stove in it where she
used to cook her dinner. She used to say "a bit of fish to go down light"
– she suffered with indigestion – but later in my life I was not surprised
because she was very much tied in at the waist and was very fat. She
was the grandmother to the little Hollands. She would sometimes give
me a bit of something she was cooking in her oven. Little did I think at
that time, that this little room would be my working room in later
years.*

*I must describe the wardrobe room at the Lyceum. It was a long room
with four windows looking on to Burleigh Street. 'The Morning Post'
office used to be at the corner and I used to look out of the windows and
see the courier on horseback arrive with despatches and tie his horse up
to what seemed to me to be the lamp-post.*

From 1882 to 1884 I was a great deal in the theatre about twice a week

49

and on Saturday matinées but on other nights I had to go to bed early. Mother was particular about this.

Edy aged 15
1884 Although I was at day school, I generally used to go down to the theatre with Mother at night. 'The Lyons Mail' used to fascinate and frighten me. Although I was in the OP corner and the actors often spoke to me as they came off, the illusion of the play was never spoilt in the least and was just as much to me as if I had been sitting in the front and had known nothing of what went on behind the scenes.

MOTHER'S ADMIRERS
1883 (Edy aged 14)
Mother had a great many admirers – especially among women – and she had a great many friends among her own sex. She used to say that women were more honest than men, as when she had lent money to men and women, that the women had always paid it back – not so with the men. Among her women admirers I can remember two particulars ones at this time – one was a Miss Eden Ramsey, who lived in Cumberland and used to send Mother lovely little boxes of lichen and flowers from her garden and used to write to her about three times a week. Another was a Miss Harries who used to do a lot of work for the Church and worked under a deaconess and was called Good Fairy, because she used to do such a lot of good deeds. We, i.e. Teddy and I always used to see the things and hear about the letters Mother received from her fans. Mother used to answer the letters she would get from her admirers. Miss Harries used to make lace with braid and used to put pins on a bit of paper and put a form against it and spray Indian ink all over it, and then later take the form up and there was a white silhouette of it left. Then she used to put the lace she had made as a border and send it as a present to Mother.

One fateful day, the deaconess, whom she had been helping, died, so as she had heard Mother was going to America, she wrote and offered to go as her secretary. Mother had never seen her and thought it would be very useful to have a secretary, so she asked her to come to see her. When Miss Harries arrived, Mother was upstairs. Looks played a very great part in Mother's likes, (Miss Ramsey was very nice-looking and we expected Miss Harries to be so). She went down and this is what she saw. A short woman with a nose like Ally Sloper, an eye like a little pig, scanty mouse-coloured hair in a long straight dress with a belt and a flounce round the bottom which just cleared her feet. Her hair was a sort of frizz and came to the bottom of her collar. Teddy and I had heard that Fairy was there and managed to be in a corner of the room for the first meeting. Mother was so taken aback that she said she had no idea of taking a secretary to America and all that she wanted was someone who would clean her boots and mend her things – not at all the kind of thing that Miss Harries would do. But to her dismay Miss Harries said she was perfectly willing to do anything she wished. Mother simply didn't know what to do and agreed to take her to America.

21. "a nose like Ally Sloper"

Ally Sloper was reputedly the first comic cartoon character, featured in a comic magazine called Ally Sloper's "Half Holiday", which was first published in 1884. Ally Sloper was a sloppy, lazy, impecunious character, forever avoiding his creditors. He wore a squashed top hat and his nose was bulbous and ugly.

EDY   *Miss Harries did everything that was wanted and managed always to be at hand when wanted and was with Mother for years. And in the end when she was too old to do any more, Mother bought her a little cottage where she lived until she died. She was most extraordinary to us. Because we were accustomed to Mother's fans being pretty people, Teddy used to make fun of her and she was very fond of him. Miss Harries never liked me because I never had much sympathy with the other fans. She was awfully good to us and when I had scarlet fever, she nursed me. Mother used to say you could never tell by a face, because she was a really good woman and most unselfish. She was also very good to animals and hired a cellar to put stray cats into when she found them but people complained so she had to cease this good work.*

Miss Harries went with Ellen to America where she was a great comfort to her. Before they left, they undertook a tour of the provinces which took place in August 1883. The dictated memoirs have several corrections of these dates.

         EDINBURGH

EDY   *Mother and Henry opened the new Lyceum Theatre August 28 1887 (should read 1883). They were the first to play there (apply to Mrs. Reed-King for the programme content)*

When we went to the theatre, planks were all across the stalls and I have never seen such a mess. Henry said "We can't possibly open" but Howard & Wyndhams said the theatre would be ready. And the play was billed to open on the 22nd but it did not open until the 23rd. When it was found that it was not possible to open on the 22nd, it was too late to tell the audience who flocked to the theatre for the opening. Bram Stoker was standing at the door when the carriages pulled up, telling them that the *theatre was not ready and that their money would be returned. We did not know it, so Eden Ramsey, Teddy and I drove up all dressed in our best. I think it was a last minute decision as the actors were all dressed but Henry said the paint was still wet and would not give a performance.*

There were several provincial tours and it is understandable that, more than fifty years later, Edy confused the dates. The opening of the Royal Lyceum Theatre in Edinburgh happened in 1883 prior to the first US tour by the Lyceum Theatre company. Henry arranged the tour to Glasgow, Edinburgh and Liverpool to make sure his transportation schedule of the scenery worked. The company, consisting of eighty persons, together with the scenery, stage properties and costumes were due to travel to America from Liverpool on a slow ship called the *City of Rome*. Henry and Ellen sailed ahead on the *Britannic*.

On October 11th 1883, huge crowds gathered on the quayside in Liverpool to see Ellen and Henry sail on the *Britannic*. Among those waving goodbye to them were Oscar Wilde and Lillie Langtry.

CHAPTER SIX

A Strange and Barbarous Land

1883

When Irving first announced that he was taking the Lyceum company on their first tour of America, Ellen Terry was terrified. The idea of crossing the Atlantic and being in that "barbarous land" made her quake with fright.

ELLEN   *"For six weeks before we started, the word America had only to be breathed to me and I burst into floods of tears! I was leaving my children, my bullfinch, my parrot, my 'aunt' Boo, whom I never expected to see alive again, just because she said I never would; and I was going to face the unknown dangers of the Atlantic and of a strange barbarous land."*

To her great surprise, Ellen was received with acclaim in America. By the time she had completed the eighth and final tour with Irving in 1901, she was equally adored on both sides of the Atlantic. She found the Americans easy to get on with, although on this first visit, she was critical of the way the women dressed. "Some of them wore Indian shawls with diamond ear-rings. They dressed too grandly in the streets and too dowdily in the theatre." But she loved the way "everyone looked happy" and described America as "a wonderful land – a land of sunshine and light, of happiness, of faith in the future."

The first tour began with a four week stay in New York where the public paid over $200,000 to see Irving and his company. The schedule was hard and every free moment was filled with dinners and parties to honour them. After New York they went by private train to Philadelphia, then on to Boston, Baltimore, then 500 miles to Brooklyn and another 1000 miles to Chicago. At first they took all the elaborate scenery they had brought with them from the Lyceum,

54

but eventually in Philadelphia, Irving came to the conclusion it was far too ambitious and so simpler staging was arranged, sometimes local carpenters working in advance of their arrival. The Chicago audiences were very responsive and Ellen later said that her performance there as Ophelia was the best she ever gave. St Louis, Cincinnati, Indianapolis and Columbus, Ohio. They encountered wintry storms, snowdrifts and ice, even a frozen Mississippi river. They braved the elements, were fêted everywhere with dinners, speeches, presentations – and yet there was time for Henry and Ellen to be alone together.

They were thrilled with their first visit to Niagara, (after that Ellen never missed visiting the Falls whenever she was in America) followed by a brief sojourn in Canada and then the final month back in New York. They returned home having made a profit of £11,700 for Irving's Lyceum management. No sooner had they arrived, when Irving began plans for a return visit to the States in September 1884. This did not leave much time for preparation for the next tour as well as for a new production of *Twelfth Night* at the Lyceum which opened on July 8th 1884.

Ellen Terry, playing Viola, became very ill at the start of the run. She had a severely poisoned thumb and was in such pain that she had to perform sitting down. Bram Stoker's brother, a doctor, visiting her backstage, realised that if nothing was done, she might have to have her arm amputated. He lanced the swelling but by then the blood poisoning in her bloodstream caused her to be very ill. She was not really fit enough to start the second tour and was quite ill and exhausted during the crossing. Irving had wisely taken the precaution of engaging Winifred Emery, a competent young understudy for her.

Back home, Ellen had left Stephen Coleridge as guardian of the children. He was a close friend and an ardent admirer of Ellen's whom she entrusted with the care of Edy and Ted, who bitterly resented him and became a real headache to his guardian.

During the second tour, Ellen was feeling particularly low. She missed her children and longed to have at least one of them with her. Rather cowardly, she could not decide which one, so she sent a cable to Stephen Coleridge saying "bring one of the children!" Edy was devastated when the Coleridges took out the 12 year old Ted. When would she be allowed to join Ellen and Henry in America?

Ellen wrote in answer to Edy's request

> *"And so America? The going to America is what you most desire? Well then, work away now!"*

Edy's only comment in her memoirs on this reads:-

> *Oct 1884 Teddy went to America with Mother and played for the first time in 'Eugene Aram' as Joey the gardener's boy – After this tour Teddy went back to school.*

22. Teddy (Edward Gordon Craig) as Joey the Gardener's Boy in "Eugene Aram"

On his return to England, Teddy went to Bradfield College, a public school where he stayed for two years, after which in 1887 he was sent to study in Heidelberg, Germany. By then he was fifteen and a very rambunctious teenager. Edy too was sent to Germany where she studied piano in Berlin with Alexis Hollander. Sadly, her long struggle with rheumatism in both hands prevented her from making music her career.

After their success in America, Henry began his plan for an elaborate production of Goethe's '*Faust*' at the Lyceum. W.G. Wills was called in to adapt it for the London stage and Henry, eager as always to create an authentic atmosphere, took a group from the Lyceum, including Ellen, the costume-designer Alice Comyns Carr and her husband John. Travelling with them were the dressers – Ellen's dresser Sally Holland and Walter Collinson, Irving's. Edy, now nearly seventeen, joined them.

EDY *In August 1885, Mother, Henry, John Comyns Carr – Alice Carr, Walter Collinson (H.I's dresser) and Sally Holland (Mother's dresser) and myself all went over to Nürenberg but we went down the Rhine and stopped to see different places. We had been seeing some beautiful castles and I shall never forget Sally Holland turning to Mother and saying "Pretty scenery, isn't it, dear?" I shall never forget Mother's face – in those days I was awfully highbrow and superior and I remember listening to the conversation between Henry and Jo Carr who were both brilliant conversationalists. Jo Carr, who had travelled a lot, was telling Henry about places where you could get special very good dishes – and I remember saying with great disgust "You two think of nothing but food". I remember being very proud because I could do something with my first two fingers. I could use them the way I had read that pickpockets could and I saw I could pick their pockets and did so – and they thought it was a great joke. A few days after that, Comyns Carr really had his pocket picked of all the money Henry had given him for the expenses. He was terribly upset and asked me if I had been playing any of my tricks (hoping I had) but I assured him that I had not. Henry was not at all upset.*

Faust opened at the Lyceum on December 19th 1885. The trip to Germany had inspired Henry with ideas for the production and he bought many objects to authenticate the props and scenery. The special effects were dramatic. The clash of swords was enhanced by real electric sparks. Indeed, one of the unfortunate actors subjected to Mephistopheles's duelling expertise, had his glove pierced and suffered an electric shock. The scenery was so elaborate that over 400 ropes were needed to shift it. Each rope had a name to help the scene shifters from making an error. Ellen, as Marguerite, took lessons in spinning and insisted on a genuine spinning wheel instead of the fake one provided.

23. Henry Irving and Ellen Terry in "Olivia" 1885

Were Henry and Ellen lovers?

It seems safe to assume they were. Three days before the opening of *Faust*, Henry wrote to her:

"No rehearsal for you this morning, my darling.
Tonight at seven dress …
It was quite amusing last night – the absolute fog of some of 'em. It will
be alright – of course – but it is a stern business.
Yes a Good drive today – perhaps you will drive down.
But do not wear yourself out – & you shall not tonight either if I can
persuade [you] to take it quietly.
What a worry you are, you see
With all my love my dearest dearest"

Faust ran until July 15, 1887, its three hundred and ninety-sixth performance. In 1886, aged seventeen, Edy played one of the angels. On Valentine's Day that year, Irving sent flowers to both Ellen and Edy.
The card read:

> *"White and red roses*
> *Sweet and fresh posies,*
> *One bunch for Edy, Angel of mine*
> *One bunch for Nell, my dear Valentine."*

We know for a fact that when Henry visited Ellen in Winchelsea and complained of having cold feet, he warmed them on her tummy. It is hard to imagine he would have enjoyed that privilege if they had been merely friends! They had to be very discreet. Ellen already had 'a reputation'. She had eloped and lived with Godwin and had two illegitimate children by him. Her marriage to Charles Kelly Wardell had resulted in a legal separation due mainly to his excessive drinking. Henry still had a very vicious wife. Any further scandal would have destroyed them both. On tour in America they were able to relax in private homes where often they were given the privacy denied them in London. They loved America so much that in August 1886 they decided to take a holiday there. Edy, aged seventeen, went with them.

EDY   *1886 August 1st*
           I went to America for the first time with Henry and Mother. We went

for a holiday to New York and Henry went to see Major Pond to arrange about his next Tour. He met other businessmen and they all went on a yacht for a "beano" and Mother and I stayed at an hotel down town, which is where the slums are now. We were there for a very short time and New York was very nearly empty. When I woke up in the morning I saw a black boy wheeling a cart full of bananas. This was most amazing to me as I had never seen so many bananas.

The heat was so great that in the horse trams the men were fanning themselves with palm leaf fans and their collars were hanging quite limp. I was sent with a letter to West 70 Street and I turned east and walked and walked until I came to the river. The little children were running about without a stitch on and the men and women sitting about. This side is the Italian Quarter and the Italians and Greeks lived in this part. The entire west was also a poor district. When I came to the river after examining everything with interest, I returned and when I found myself in 5th Avenue I made straight for the hotel which was near Washington Square and didn't try to find the place anymore.

I went on the elevated railway and was most interested to look into all the rooms. I was taken round by General Porter – he was a general in the North and South War and he showed me all the sights of New York.

We went to Narragansett, a seaside place. This is where I first met Miss Urquhart and her sister Mrs. Brown-Potter, (they were the Belles of the place) and Sally Fairchild and a great friend of Mother's, Mrs. Lockwood who she had met when she was in America before. The fashion then was for the older people to dine out together and the younger people all dined together. I was thrown in with the Lockwood girls. People in America always seemed to begin the conversation about the Immortal Soul, Browning etc. Everyone talked at once and no one seemed to listen. Someone suddenly turned to me and said "What is your opinion?" to which I replied "I am sorry but I don't think I have got one". This obviously was not the right answer but as everyone was talking, it didn't matter very much. I was not accustomed to going out to dinner without Mother and afterwards I told Mother how terrifying it had all been – and she laughed very much.

After being at Narragansett which was for about a week, I returned to New York and England.

CHAPTER SEVEN

A Death, a Confirmation – Scotland and Germany

1886 Edy aged 17

Soon after their return home, Edy's father, Edward Godwin fell ill. His health had always been poor. The excruciating pain of kidney stones eventually forced his doctors to recommend an operation, a risky procedure in those days. His wife, Beatrice was in Paris when his friends realised that Godwin's condition was serious, so they sent for her. He never recovered and died just before midnight on 6th October 1886. Beatrice and his good friend Whistler and Lady Archibald Campbell were with him at the end. He was 53 years old.

Very early the next morning, Whistler walked to the home of the artist Louise Joplin to ask her to undertake the difficult task of breaking the news to Ellen Terry. Mrs Joplin was a beautiful brunette, immortalised by Millais. She knew Ellen well, having painted a portrait of her. Whistler and Joplin felt it would be unthinkable for Ellen to read of Godwin's death in the newspaper. Happy and relaxed after her holiday with Henry and Edy in America, Ellen was devastated by the news. In her memoirs, Louise Joplin wrote that she would never forget that grief-stricken cry "There was no one like him!" Godwin's funeral was bizarre. His body was buried near Whitney in Oxfordshire. His coffin was placed on a farm wagon which carried him, Whistler, Beatrice and Lady Campbell to his requested last resting place "in a corner of a field". Two years later Beatrice and Whistler were married.

Barred from going to Godwin's funeral because of the impropriety of their relationship, Ellen had to grieve in private. Following so soon after the death of her ex-husband Charles Kelly Wardell, the death of her lover seemed to strip Ellen of all her natural joy in living. She became miserable and depressed. She continued her work but her heart was not in it. On the verge of a complete nervous breakdown, she decided to send for Edy.

EDY   *While I was at Dixter in 1886, in the month of October, my father died and Mother sent for me to go up to London. The Mallesons told me I must be very nice to Mother.*

Ellen later confessed that she had been selfish and wrong to take Edy out of school that October, but by Christmas she was feeling better and "I am alright now," she wrote. "Edith did that".

Ellen had high ambitions for Edy's further education. Countless letters from her mother encouraged her to study hard so that she could gain entrance to Girton College, much favoured by Mrs Malleson. To Ellen's chagrin, Edy did not pass the entrance examination. Ellen urged her to have a second try but Edy was not going to be coerced into that again.

EDY   *I had worked for the Higher Local Examination Oxford and had failed. I think Mother had an idea that it would be nice if I went to one of the universities – but I didn't mind failing in the least, but it was a great disappointment to Mother. I got ploughed for such curious things, viz. Shakespeare, spelling and writing. My Shakespeare was so original and I knew such a lot about his plays, all of which was not in the textbooks, that I failed. I was not at all surprised about spelling as I have never been able to spell. My Bible knowledge got full marks and I put that down to a special reason. I was staying with Stanley Lane Pool and his brother, Reginald Pool, who were making a revised version of the Bible. Reginald Pool was a Don at Oxford and the husband of Rachel Malleson and I used to go to stay with them at Oxford.*

In January 1887 I was confirmed by the Bishop Bickersteth of Exeter, all by myself, as Mr. Barnes, who was the former Prebendary Bishop of Exeter (Violet and Irene Vanbrugh's father) had given me a note to him. Miss Harries went with me. The Bishop was very nice to me and told me about a daughter he had had called Edith who had died. I went and had tea in the Bishop's drawing room. There was a door by which you could go into the cathedral without going out. I had white gloves for my confirmation and could not enjoy my tea much because I didn't know what was going to happen.

Directly after this I went with Mabel Malleson to Heidelberg until July 1887. Then I came back for the holidays in Scotland.

MUSIC STUDIES
LEONARD BORWICK – distinguished pianist 1868-1925
EDY   *I had music lessons from the same master as he did, when he was wearing knickerbockers suits. I always used to say "How is the little boy?" and Mr. Bird the music master used to say "Very well" but he used to say "You don't work". I was rather envious of the little boy as I wanted to play well – but I was lazy and did not work.*

In spite of this self-deprecating report, Edy inherited her father's love of music and played the piano quite well. Refusing to try again for Girton, Edy decided instead to further her musical studies. Ellen gave in and sent her to Berlin to study piano with Alexis Hollander. Mabel Malleson accompanied her to keep an eye on her. Teddy meanwhile was sent to Heidelberg College where his behaviour was reprehensible. He skipped lessons, smoked and culminated his exploits by absconding at night and exploring the countryside on his bicycle. Edy's behaviour too, although not in the same category, gave Mabel some anxious moments.

HEIDELBERG
EDY   *After this I went to Heidelberg – where I went with Mabel Malleson. I loved this. We stayed in a Pension with a Professor Müller. I liked the Germans but did not like the professor's two daughters. I loved the winter*

when we went skating on the flood water from the Neckar. They had torch light and fires at the sides and delicious things used to be cooked, such as sticky chestnuts and bits of meat and sausages all cooked on skewers. They were delicious and you ate them off the skewers. It was all very bright and gay and crowds of students were there. Professor Müller had a large home and let rooms to a lot of students and we lived en pension and used to spend the evenings together. There was one, Doctor Mieda, a Japanese – he was a medical student. He was an exceptional little man and used to do the most minute operations. His bedroom was next to mine and I was once awakened in the early morning by hearing an awful row. He was having a party and they had all got very drunk and someone fell against my door which burst the door open as one of his guests fell in head first. It was quite dark but the light shone into my room from the door. There was a general hush as he was pulled out by the legs. I liked the Japanese very much.

There was one little theatre. I had one seat there every week – the same seat on the same night. It was very cheap – about 2/- (two shillings) *a time. We had light operas, plays, comedies, tragedies – in fact they catered for the students. The great amusement was to see the different students swaggering in. The Russians were the most swaggers.* [sic] *They wore white caps – which they had to earn in some way. Then they had a riband which they wore across the shoulder. The ribands were different colours and they belonged to different corps. The different corps used to fight each other. They used to fight with a very large and unwieldy sword, bigger than a claymore. They had heavy gauntlets and padded coats and the only part that was exposed was the face. It was grand to have a cut on the face and some of the students used to rub salt and red wine into their cuts. They also used to wear fobs which they earned by drinking. When they could drink a huge bock (drinking mug) slowly – you got a fob and you always had to shut the lid unless it was empty.*

Heidelberg Ice Festival
They flooded a field alongside the river – there were banks all the way

round. They had it well lit up and braziers and they used to cook a kind of pancake – also bits of meat on skewers and lovely Christmas sugared and toffee apples. People used to always go at night in their smartest skating costumes. I was never any good at skating because my ankles were not strong enough but there were chairs with red braid and were on runners and you were pushed about.

We used to go sleigh-riding which was lovely. There was a most beautiful old castle that used to be illuminated on certain occasions and we all used to go up there on festas. It had beautiful octagonal towers at each corner. On one occasion I dressed up as a student in a big coat and a fur cap. I had to tuck my hair up into it as it was long and I wore the fur cap because it was kept on all the time and if I had had another I should have had to take it off – and you always carried your walking stick head downward in your pocket. I got up after Mabel Malleson and I had gone to bed. I used to get up and used to go over the balcony. Mabel woke up during the night and took my clothes away. Mabel had taken them. She brought them in in the morning. I thought she would be cross but she could not hide her amusement and said she had seen me come in and that I looked very nice. She had to write to Mother about it however and I think after that I left Heidelberg. Then I came back for the holidays in Scotland.

SCOTLAND 1887

Ellen's elder sister, Kate Terry Lewis had made a good marriage. Arthur Lewis was a wealthy man, a partner in Lewis and Allenby in Conduit Street. Their home was Moray Lodge, a magnificent house, which, like Little Holland House where Ellen had lived with Watts, bordered the Holland Estate. Arthur Lewis loved nothing more than to welcome artists and musicians to his home and Kate, like the Pattle sisters, ruled in her own little court from where, at that time, as she was still living with Godwin, her younger sister Ellen and her two illegitimate children were banned. When Ellen married Charles Kelly Wardell, however, all was forgiven and they were welcomed at Kate's homes in both London and Scotland.

EDY

August 1887 Edy aged 17

I made my first visit to Scotland. I went up to Aunt Kate's which – [sic]
*We went by train to Inverness and I travelled up for the first time in a
sleeper which was most exciting. We went to Glen Urquhart in a carriage
and Mother got me a Glen Urquhart plaid Inverness cape – I think she
bought a huge bale of this stuff – I remember it used to haunt us for
years. We went to the mill where it was made – it is a lovely grey with
darker grey criss-crosses.*

*It was the first time that I had been in a large house with heaps of
servants, carriages and horses etc but they lead what I call a 'Town Life'
in Scotland. My cousins were not allowed to run wild. They used to walk
and walk over the moors. There were lovely little waterfalls and I loved
the look of these things but I hated the house. The house was one storey.
There were twelve of us and crowds of servants. It was furnished
'Victorian-Scots' and the gravel was all kept rolled. The curtains were
tartan and tartan tablecloths. We drove a lot, and with two lovely horses,
dappled greys. I used to like going out for these drives. Aunt Kate was
very fat and never walked and Mother never walked (but she was very
thin) so I used to get the chance of going with them which I loved.*

*On the way back from Aunt Kate's, we stayed at No.5 Melville Street,
Edinburgh. Eden Ramsey (she was one of Mother's admirers) had asked
us to go to stay there. Mother, I think, went to the hotel. Boo brought
Teddy up to Edinburgh and he and I stayed with Eden Ramsey and I
think Boo stayed with Mother in rooms in Melville Street. I was very
interested because everything was covered. The furniture was covered in
chintz. I liked it very much. It was glazed and the furniture in our new
house was the latest thing in advanced art – it was belonging to the
aesthetic period and I had never come across this kind of old-
fashionedness which I rather liked.*

*After Edinburgh we went to the Royalty Theatre Glasgow. There was a
fire there. Henry and I were the only people there and Sally was getting*

Mother's things ready. The Pit and Gallery largely composed of students were in and singing heartily. They never knew of the fire. Three of the scenes of 'Faust' were destroyed before they could get out. I remember wondering what to save and took all Mother's brushes and Sally her washing which had just arrived. Loveday was a poor little man who always seemed to have indigestion. I was so surprised to see him go dashing up a ladder or rope to tear down some blazing scenery. He was our Stage Manager.

Sarah Bernhardt had taken the Lyceum Theatre in London while Henry and Mother were in Edinburgh.

1887
I went on tour. We got back to London in October.
Mother was ill.

1888 Heringsdorf

At the end of the 19th century the little German village Heringsdorf developed into a luxurious and very popular holiday resort. In 1888 it was still unspoilt, when Ellen and Edy took a brief break there.

EDY   *It was a little tiny visit to the north of Germany. We used to spend hours on the beach collecting amber, getting quite big knobs. I am not sure that we were not there in the spring. There seemed to be no other people there and there were sand dunes. We had a lovely holiday there. I think we went with Nanny Held (Anna Held) and Mother, but not Teddy. I think he had gone to Heidelberg. He went to a preparatory school chiefly for army young men.*

It was in autumn 1888 that Teddy was expelled from Heidelberg College following a somewhat seedy exploit with a local girl. The sign of things to come?

EDY'S MEMORIES OF LONDON IN 1887

Clare Market

> *Which Kingsway has swept away. It was a shade further east than Kingsway and there you seemed to be able to get anything. It was like the market in Farringdon Street. If anything was wanted at the theatre, they always used to say "run round to Clare Market!" It was a very great loss when it went.*

Seven Dials

> *The houses there had all cages and cages of little wild birds and animals. The paths were very narrow and covered in mud and the people about there were very tough – I used to love going up there.*

Wardour Street

> *You used to be able to get imitations of nearly anything quite cheap – it was a great help for the theatre – you could get suits of armour, chains, mummies etc., etc., the things used to be outside the shops.*

Booksellers Row

> *Which used to run between St Clement Danes to St Mary Le Strand and on the south side of the churches there was a butcher's shop with rows and rows of Welsh mutton hanging up spattered with mud – it was just like a toy butcher's shop.*

Electric Light

> *The first electric light was on Waterloo Bridge and along the embankment – we rushed down to see it.*

Statue of Florence Nightingale in Lower Regent Street by Walker

> *Erected 1913, three years after her death. The dress that Florence Nightingale is depicted in was lent by me. It is the one that Mother wore in her very last appearance on any stage.*

CHAPTER EIGHT

My Second Visit to America

Oct 1887 Edy aged 18

EDY *In the Autumn of 1887 I went to America for the second time on the 'Britannic'. I don't remember much about the voyage except that I was ill the whole way – I am an awful sailor! We went to four places – New York – Philadelphia – Chicago and Boston and finished the tour in March 1888.*

The first thing that Mother pointed out to me was Brooklyn Bridge which looked as if it was made of thread. It was so high and at that time I believe it was the biggest suspension bridge in the world. There were no skyscrapers in those days in New York and I was not very much impressed. I went to a great many theatres as I was not playing.

Harrigan and Hart
These were two actors that used to act in Downtown in dramas. I liked them very much. I very distinctly remember one play which was Irish 'Miss Yeomans'. There was an Irish wedding in which there was singing and dancing. She returned to her bedroom and for some reason which I cannot remember, decided to take poison and she was very tragic and instead of taking poison, she made a mistake and took whisky in her wedding veil and orange blossom. She got drunker and drunker always thinking she was dying. It was the funniest thing I ever saw.

Mother and Henry were playing 'The Merchant of Venice', 'Faust', 'Olivia' and 'Lyons Mail'.

At Philadelphia I was very impressed by the houses – white marble everywhere – marble about six feet up and then red brick. The nice houses were Georgian. Tramcars drawn by horses on very narrow streets. The theatre was in this narrow street and was called Chestnut Street Opera House. The streets were named by the trees which had been planted at the corners. This was originally definitely a puritan settlement. Mother knew very nice people there. One of the things I noticed – that the hotel we stayed in was considered the latest thing and by the next time we visited the town, another hotel was the latest and the one we had formerly stayed in was considered downtown and had sometimes degenerated into tenements.

While there, I used often to go and spend the day with a friend of Mother's, a Mrs. Golespu. She was a descendant of Benjamin Franklin. She was a very great character – a very strong type of American woman – not smart at all. There I had for the first time real American cooking (before that in the hotels it was always French). We had "planked shad" Shad, which was a fish – was put upon an oaken plank and cooked over the fire. It got smokey from the taste of the oak smoke. It was served on the piece of oak – the oak was about 2 inches thick, I think and about 18 ins x 12 ins I was very interested in it but don't remember liking it particularly.

In each of the towns I came into quite a different life. In this they wore plain clothes and had American dishes – it was very clean and fresh – white collars and cuffs etc. In Philadelphia the people were not very well off.

Chicago was the supreme top notch of the Middle West. We made a great many friends there and they were chiefly very well-to-do. They were very hospitable. When we went into our rooms at the hotel, we could see that our friends had been in, arranging the calendars on the desks, flowers in every conceivable corner etc. Chicago is beautifully situated on Lake Michigan. The people there were the supreme top-notch of society in the

Middle West. In Chicago you were always entertained to lunch parties but no men came to them – always women. The houses were all heated and you always wore your hot Garden Party clothes.

Henry was entertained to supper. In each town they generally had a Farewell Supper at which Mother, Henry [sic]. I also used to go with Mother. I used to like the supper parties very much. I learnt to eat oysters for the first time. They were small. I thought I didn't like them before. Once I had been given half a one at an oyster bed – it was the wrong half and I did not like it at all.

At one house we visited for a lunch party, the window looked over the lake. All the women were dressed up to the nines. The clothes were sent from Paris. The only quietly dressed woman who was there and she looked very nice was Mrs. Cleveland, the wife of Mr. Cleveland sometime President. The others were dressed in rose pink velvets and white satin loaded with thousands of pounds of jewellery. The lady next to me, who was dressed in turquoise blue, was the wife of the proprietor of the best store – in fact the second biggest in America. She told me they were going to open a store in London in Oxford Street and plied me with questions about it. I asked her if it was near Oxford Circus and Cambridge Circus but she did not seem to know and seemed to think it was more to the west. In those days there were very poky little shops in that part, but I didn't like to tell her this as she seemed to think it was somewhere near Buckingham Palace. The shop proved to be Selfridges and on consideration, it is May Fair? Or very near it.

The lady in turquoise was the wife of Harry Gordon Selfridge, who at that time was the manager of Marshall Field in Chicago, which today is part of the Macy's empire. His aim was to build an American department store in London and it was actually in his retirement that his dream came true. When he laid the foundation stone in 1908, he described it as "the greatest moment in my life". One year after the foundations were laid, the huge building was finished.

EDY

Boston, from my point of view, meant the Fairchilds. We were there in January 1888. It was not so American as the other places and there were houses that reminded me of Park Lane and the streets were not straight. There were trees on the Common and it was an old place. The architecture was mixed. We lived in a Hotel not far from the Fairchilds – and I was sent over to have lunch by myself. I did not know it at the time but Mrs. Fairchild telephoned Mother to know what I could eat as we had come to the fourth course and I hadn't eaten anything. I was most suspicious as I did not know what any of the things were and I never wanted to try new things.

First there was clam broth in little cups – which I had never had before and didn't know how to manage. There were curious things that I was never accustomed to. Poor Mrs. Fairchild was very upset as she thought if people didn't like the things, there was something wrong with them, which made her very unhappy.

The Fairchilds
There were seven in the family – two girls Sally and Lucia – the latter painted – Charlie – Jack – Neil – Blair and Gordon. Charlie was at Harvard and Jack was going there. Sally and I went to look at Jack's room to see if it would be all right and where a bath could be put in. I was so struck with the size of the baths – they had very high short ones in some cases and I remember the one he had went into a sort of cupboard.

Gordon, who was the youngest and had curls and wore a kilt, asked me if I liked soda water (which meant icecream soda). I thinking of "sweps" [sic.] said 'No' and his expression was incredulous. Sally and I became 'chums'. In every town in America there is always a Chinese shop and a Japanese shop. Sally and I used always to be going to them. We loved them and got many things in there.

Edy's New York debut was in *Barbara* by Jerome K. Jerome. Using her stage name Ailsa Craig, she played the part of Barbara in this New York production on 26 March 1888.

EDY   *1888 In New York I played a leading part in some amateur theatricals entitled 'Barbara'. I acted it with a friend of mine whom I had known in England. We did it in a downtown sort of place but had a very distinguished audience – Mother, Henry Irving, John Sargent etc., etc. The play was for some scheme downtown – I have forgotten what it was for. I was awfully nervous. I didn't mind going on doing anything as long as I didn't have to speak, but if I had to speak, I was terrified. I was and have always had the greatest difficulty to memorise anything.*

Horace Howard Furness (1833 –1912) was the most important American Shakespearean scholar of the 19th century.

EDY   *In New York I went with Mother and Mr. Furness – he was a great authority on Shakespeare and he had one of Shakespeare's gloves in a glass case. I remember feeling that his glove ought not to be in America.*

Henry Ward Beecher was the brother of Harriet Beecher Stowe, author of Edy's childhood favourite *Uncle Tom's Cabin*. A charismatic, outspoken clergyman, he advocated women's suffrage and deplored slavery. His fiery colourful sermons were attended by Abraham Lincoln and Mark Twain, the latter describing him as "sawing his arms in the air, howling sarcasms this way and that, discharging rockets of poetry and exploding mines of eloquence, halting now and then to stamp his foot three times in succession to emphasize a point." Ward Beecher even toured England during the Civil War to explain the strategies of the North.

Tragedy struck when Henry Ward Beecher was accused of adultery with Elizabeth Tilton, the wife of one of his parishioners. The scandal resounded round the entire country and everyone followed the intrigues of the trial that lasted over six months. His loyal wife stood by him throughout, and eventually the jury acquitted him and he continued to preach until March 8th 1887 when he died from a sudden cerebral haemorrage. Mrs Henry Ward Beecher was still reeling from her loss when Ellen and Edy went to lunch with her later that year.

EDY   *1st November 1887 I met Mrs Henry Ward Beecher. She was very strict and narrow and hated actresses – but she adored Mother and Mother was very fond of her. She had met her the year before. She lived in New York. She told us all about her husband's death and was very much moved by her account.*

            In 1887 I saw Wagner's 'Tristan' for the first time. We didn't like it very much.

24. Ada Rehan and John Drew in "The Railroad of Love"

Ada Rehan and John Drew were acting in 'Railroad of Love' at Daly's Theatre — we went and had supper with them after seeing their show, at Del Monico's — it was the great place for eating and I enjoyed it very much.

John Drew was the uncle of John, Ethel and Lionel Barrymore and the great-great-uncle of Drew Barrymore. He was an adored matinée idol and a fine Shakespearian actor as well as excelling in comedy and society drama of the day. However, Ellen was ecstatic about the acting of his leading lady, Ada Rehan.

25. Clara Morris

ELLEN *The Daly players were a revelation to me of the pitch of excellence which American acting had reached. My first night at Daly's was an enchantment. I wrote to Mr. Daly and said: "You've got a girl in your company who is the most lovely humorous darling I have ever seen on the stage." It was Ada Rehan. Now of course, I didn't 'discover' her or any rubbish of that kind; the audience were already mad about her, but I did know her for what she was, even in that brilliant "all star" company and before she had played in the classics and won enduring fame. The audacious superb quaint Irish creature! Never have I seen such splendid high comedy…*

I also saw 'Dorothy' which was then played in America for the first time. François Cellier conducted. He went out on the same boat as we did. I had already seen it in London and liked it very much.

EDY *We also knew Clara Morris — I thought she was wonderful. I remember her telling me in the dressing room that she had been ill in bed and she wanted to see Mother and Henry acting on their first visit to America. She had been ordered by the doctor not to get up, but when she was left alone, she got up, wrapped something round her shoulders, and climbed out on to the roof, from whence she could get on to the theatre roof and from there she got into the back of the gallery and saw Mother and H.I. act.*

Josef Hofmann the legendary pianist was without doubt "one of the best", as Edy described him. He was not only a virtuoso pianist, but also an inventor. Windscreen wipers, shock absorbers, a house that revolved to face the sun, were just a few of his seventy patented inventions. He had very small hands and so designed a special piano with narrower keys to enable him to stretch an octave and more. He had a keen sense of humour. My late husband, Ezra Rachlin who was studying with Hofmann, was called to his studio one day to play for him. Ezra could not understand why he was playing so many wrong notes. Then Hofmann laughed and pointed to the other piano in the studio, explaining that he had tricked his young student by asking him to play on the piano with the narrower keys! Hofmann became Dean of the famous Curtis Institute of Music in Philadelphia where his pupils included Jeanne Behrend, Abbey Simon, Leonard Bernstein, Abram Chasins, Shura Cherkassky, William Harms, Harry Kaufman, Ezra Rachlin, Nadia Reisenberg and several other of the most talented young students of the day.

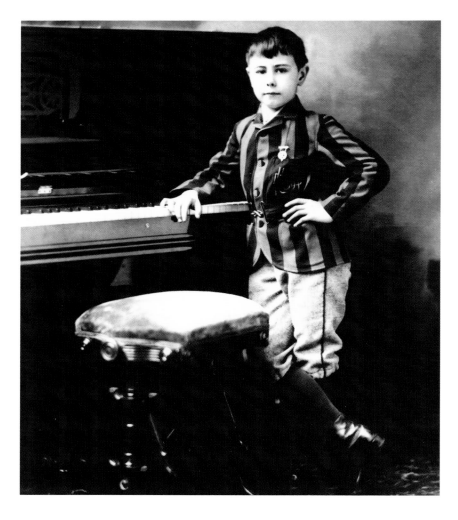

26. Josef Hofmann

EDY *Josef Hofmann as a little boy was also in New York and was attracting huge audiences as a child. We went to one of his concerts. He was very good and I think he is one of the best.*

 He came home on the same boat with his mother and father. We knew him by that time. He went about on the boat with a pencil and paper, getting people to promise to do something in a concert programme he was getting up and he came and asked Henry if he would recite. He, Henry rubbed up his hair the wrong way and said "Run away, little boy!" and Hofmann replied "I am not speaking to you as a little boy but as a fellow artist." Of course, Henry recited after that.

In 1890 Edy attended the Royal Academy of Music where, in March, she took a Trinity College London Examination in piano. Although she passed the examination, her marks were not high enough to encourage her to pursue a professional career as a musician. This was largely due to the arthritis in her hands that was to be a problem all her life.

The stage beckoned and it was later that year that she had her first professional speaking role as Polly Flamborough in *Olivia* at the Grand Theatre Islington which had a capacity of three thousand people. Little wonder she was nervous!

CHAPTER NINE

Mischief Afoot!

EDY ON STAGE

Apart from a list of the plays in which she appeared, little was known of Edith Craig the actress. As a member of Irving's Lyceum company, she played Jessica in *The Merchant of Venice* in 1895, a year in which she also appeared as Sozel in *The Bells*, a Maid in Pinero's *Bygones* and a niece in *The Lyons Mail*. In 1900 Shaw chose her to play Proserpine Garnett in *Candida* at the Strand Theatre, in which role she also went on tour. She acted in Ellen Terry's own productions of Ibsen's *The Vikings* and Christopher St John's translation of *The Good Hope*. Her memoirs reveal that, whereas she was nervous and suffered from extreme stagefright, she was also mischievous and full of fun on stage. Ellen had a great sense of humour and often had a problem controlling her laughter on stage, particularly when making a mistake. What we know now from Edy's reminiscences, is how many times she resorted to playful pranks to relieve the boredom of being a 'super'! Sometimes her wicked sense of humour backfired when her mother was in the middle of a dramatic Shakespearian scene. We now meet a very different Edy from the strict disciplinarian described by so many who worked under her direction in later years.

EDY   *In 1885 I was a super in 'Olivia'.*
My first part that I ever played – Grand Theatre Islington 1890 Polly Flamborough in 'Olivia'. Mother didn't know if I was going to disgrace myself. Old Loveday, the stage manager, when it came to the question of what I should be called, took up a directory and put his finger on the name Hallet and I was called Miss Hallet in the cast. This was at the Grand Theatre Islington. I shook all over and got my words out but was pretty bad. I think

Norman Forbes was in it. Altogether I played three different parts in 'Olivia', Polly Flamborough, Sophia and The Gipsy. When I was playing this part in New York, my mother, Henry Irving and myself went to the Edison place and made a record. He gave us a little wax cylinder, which we could play. I was secretly awfully pleased with myself when I heard it but Henry said "Is that awful sound me?" Mother came out very well. The Edison place was a scientific place and they were doing experiments. I think this was the first year that I ever saw a motor car. It looked like a wagonette with a high box in the front and a wheel and it had a bell like a fire engine – but no man walked in front of it with a red flag as they did in this country.

In 1888 when Ellen received the news that Teddy had been expelled from Heidelberg College, she was shocked to read that her son had exasperated the staff to such an extent that they declared he had "a very ill-disciplined nature with an impulsive temper." After attempts to discipline him by sending him to study Shakespeare with the Revd Mr Gorton, a recognised expert, Ellen was pleased when Irving invited both Teddy and Edy to join the company at the Lyceum Theatre. Edward Gordon Craig made his first appearance in 1889, playing Ellen's son in *The Dead Heart*, by Watts Phillips.

27. Edward Gordon (Teddy) Craig in *The Dead Heart* (1889)

1889 aged 20

EDY *I remember going with Teddy to the Private View. It was when he was acting in 'Dead Heart'. He was wearing his first top hat and frock coat and looked very good. I always had one best dress each year and I always wore it for the first time at The New Gallery as this visit was always a great occasion to me.*

In the papers it said "Gordon Craig and his sister were among those at the Private View". I resented this. I had been "Ellen Terry and her daughter" – this I didn't mind but I resented it when I was called "sister". I didn't realize it at the time but Teddy was almost a matinée idol, being very good looking.

December 9th 1890 21st Birthday (not 12th as written)

Henry Irving gave me a party on the Lyceum stage. I think they were playing 'The Corsican Brothers' at the time. He had a huge horseshoe table on the stage and Henry sat at one point of the horseshoe and Mother at the other and I sat in the middle at the top. Aunt Kate, Uncle Arthur, Mabel and Lucy, Floss and Mr. Morris and Fred and Marion. Aunt Kate sat next to Henry, and General Thesiger and Lord Winchelsea sat on either side of Mother. Justin McCarthy and Edie Lane on either side of me, Sir Frederic Haynes who was a devoted admirer of Marion's and every week wherever she was he always used to send her a box of flowers. [sic] He wore his whiskers brushed forward and was covered with medals. He had lost an eye in the Crimean War. Alfred Parsons, Alfred Austin, Johnston Forbes Robertson, Graham Robertson, the Alexanders, the Casellas, the Coleridges, the Bram Stokers, the Comyn Carrs, Miss Harries. We had 'Chirgwin the White-Eyed Kaffir' as an entertainment. Lady Winchelsea and Paul Cooper were also there. I had a new evening dress for the occasion, made of yellow satin trimmed with buttercups. Everyone made beautiful speeches of course. The women didn't speak and Justin McCarthy returned thanks for me. Women didn't speak in those days.

G.H. Chirgwin was always billed as The White-Eyed Kaffir. He specialized in songs with witty lyrics and wise-cracking humour. He was perfect after-dinner entertainment and always blacked up, with a white diamond over one eye.

1892 Dec 3, St James's Theatre *Liberty Hall.*

28. Edith Craig (striped dress) in *Liberty Hall*

Maude Millett as Amy Chilworth, Ben Webster as Hon. Gerald Harringay, Edith Craig as Miss Hickson, Edward Righton as William Todman, H.H. Vincent as Mr J. Briginshaw and possibly Alfred Holles as Mr Hickson in *Liberty Hall*, St James's Theatre.

EDY   *1892 December 3rd St James' Theatre*
           My first London engagement in the first night of a new London play
           'Liberty Hall' by R.C. Carton. I had three lines and got quite good
           notices and a letter from the author.

Even in those early days I was keen on costume and asked if I might be allowed to go up into the wardrobe and choose the clothes I wanted so that they would not have to buy new ones. I got a rather good character make-up with particularly characteristic Prunella boots with elastic sides – a striped silk dress with a plastron of lace (which I supplied myself) a long gold chain with the ends tucked into a petersham belt and long gold earrings, hair parted in the middle and screwed into a little knot at the back. I was only on in the one scene and during the action we had to sit at a card table and I, being the least important of the quartet, was put with my back to the audience. After the play had been running some time, I got rather bored with this bit and thought I would vary it with a little bit of by-play. I had always lifted my skirt when I sat at the card table so as to show my Prunella boots but this time one evening while Mr. Ben Wilshe and Miss Maude Millett were having a love scene, and we were all four playing cards with our noses in the cards, I just threw up my feet with my toes together with my heels apart – the boots I think were more 8s than 7s and I was quite unprepared for the roar of laughter that went up. I became absolutely rigid and paralysed and could not move. (George) Alexander and Marion Terry who were floating about at the back said "Is it a cat? – has anybody come undone?" But I never let on what it really was and no one would ever have known if I could have resisted doing it again. After it had happened a second time, Maude Millett sent someone round to sit in front to see what it really was – and then the fat was in the fire but I had had great fun out of it.

Later on in that same show, I was driving with Mother in the park, Alexander was riding in the Row and he stopped the carriage and said "You have not got my telegram! You are playing Maude Millett's part at the Crystal Palace this afternoon (I was her understudy). I had only been given the understudy because Maude Millett had never been known to be ill and if you said in the profession that you were her understudy, it was treated with derision. I went home at once and tried to get some of the words into my head and went gaily off to the Crystal Palace. In the play

I spoke the first line. Luckily I had to speak to Ben Webster (who is one of the kindest people on the stage to nervous actresses with little experience) so he had warned me of the double echo of the Crystal Palace and after I had said my first line and heard it come back to me from the different parts of the audience, I began perfectly gibbering and could not go on at all and he pulled me through. After the Crystal Palace, it was quite easy playing it at the St James's, which I did, I think, for about a week.

29. Maude Millett (Mrs Tennant)

Maude Millett, who was amazingly good-looking and the adored of all the university students and young men of the town, was possessed of a very hearty appetite and she had indulged too freely in pork, which was the cause of her illness and when she came back I had prepared a pleasant surprise for her. I had cut out dozens of little pigs out of orange peel and

*whatever she did, she found one, and wherever she looked she saw one –
she became so hysterical with laughing that in her serious scene when she
elopes with the young man, she could hardly go on.*

'The Two Orphans' at the Adelphi Theatre May 12 to June 18th 1894.

*This was a revival and I played one of the grand naughty ladies of the
Court and also later on was in prison. I had to teach them all how to
dance the minuette [sic] and I taught them fencing. I always had to
teach dancing and fencing as I learnt to fence when I was young. It was
there that I was supposed to have laughed in the prison scene. (Miss Alma
Stanley was in the cast) I was sacked. I walked round to the Lyceum and
met William Terriss who was awfully enraged and wanted to go round
and see the man and kick him, but Mother wouldn't let him. On Ascot
Night, the whole company was so drunk that I had to hold up a lot of
them and I was really the well-behaved member of the Company.*

ANGELO'S FENCING ACADEMY

Henry Charles Angelo the younger (1780-1852), grandson of the original Angelo,
held the position of fencing master and superintendent of sword exercises in the
army. He moved the Academy to 32 St. James's Street (1830-1896)

EDY   *I used to go to this school for fencing and gymnasium.
This was the great place in the 18th century and in the room in which
we used to fence, there were very interesting prints and pictures – many
of Chevalier d'Eon de Beaumont who had learnt fencing from Angelo –
in this room which was bare of all furniture. The building was in St
James's Street and you went down a passage and up three steps where
there was a little room that you changed in. Down below in a place that
I think was the basement, there were horses and parallel bars and ropes
attached to the ceiling. I found that I could climb these ropes with no
trouble as I didn't have to use my feet. I always had trouble with my feet
and was afraid on ladders and stairs.*

30. Eugene Sandow

The fencing we did upstairs and many actors used to come to rub up their fencing here. I found that the double joints in my arms were very useful as they allowed me to get a better reach.

I do not know if it was because the last of the Angelos died, but the place was ultimately sold to Sandow (Eugene – first bodybuilder and strongman on the stage circa 1897) *and once, when I was passing later, I felt I must look in and oh! it was all changed. I went down the passage, which was now tiled and not so long as it used to be, because a glass door had been put up. I pushed this open and was confronted by three men standing on a plush carpet, with spats and button holes, who came forward and wished to know if they could do anything for me. I asked them if they taught fencing there as I used to learn there. They said that physical culture was taught. I asked if I could go in and when I did so, I found a great change. Turkish carpets, curtains, gold chairs etc. I saw Sandow in ordinary clothes which do not become a highly developed athlete. He looked very fine in fleshings, striking an attitude with the limelight on him – but in ordinary clothes – no!*

In 1897 Sandow created the Institute of Physical Culture, an early gymnasium for body builders.

1896 AILSA CRAIG – CAUSE OF CHANGE OF NAME

As an actress, most people knew Edy by her stage name Ailsa Craig. In September 1883 when Ellen Terry was on holiday with Ted and Irving, she saw the famous Ailsa Craig rock off the Ayrshire coast of Scotland. "What a good stage name!" she cried. "Pity you can't have it, Ted, I shall give it to Edy". But it was not Edy's first stage name – nor her last! She had three altogether! We now know that it was a gossiping theatrical landlady who was the real reason why Edy abandoned the name Ailsa Craig.

LODGING HOUSE KEEPERS
1896 Ailsa Craig

EDY   *If you talked at all to some of these, they used to think they were your greatest friends. On one occasion my mother went to stay at some rooms that I had had. The landlady produced a newspaper cutting which she showed Mother on which was the announcement of the coming marriage of a Miss Ailsa Craig – but said that she couldn't believe that it was true because I had never told her anything about it.*

The lady in question was on the stage, but I think in rather a different line of work. On one occasion she met an actor who was a friend of my Uncle Fred but who didn't know me. They met in a bar of a Brighton hotel and she became very friendly with him, when he said he knew my Uncle Fred, she owned the relationship and they had several drinks together. I gather that she got rather cheeky and somehow or other upset him. He, meeting my Uncle Fred the next day, advised him to speak to me and advise me not to get so fresh with strangers in the bar. My uncle, apart from not recognising the type, knew that I was at that moment on tour in Scotland, was able to prove an alibi by proxy. Nevertheless my uncle handed the story in to me and advised me to change my first name, so I took my second which is Edith. But I followed the career of my namesake in the police news and society columns with a certain amount of interest.

Tour with Independent Theatre, July 1897 First tour by myself – first time I played in Shaw and Ibsen. See Shaw/Terry letters page 234-237)

In the opening scene of *Candida*, The Revd. James Morell has a secretary Prossy, played by Edy, whom Shaw described as

"The typist, Miss Proserpine Garnett, is a brisk little woman of about 30, of the lower middle class, neatly but cheaply dressed in a black merino skirt and a blouse, rather pert and quick of speech, and not very civil in her manner, but sensitive and affectionate. She is clattering away busily at her machine whilst Morell opens the last of his morning's letters. He realises its contents with a comic groan of despair."

EDY   *They sent out 'Candida' and 'A Doll's House'. Through Shaw I got the part of Prossy (Proserpine) in 'Candida' and also had to play Mrs. Linden in 'A Doll's House'. We went on tour starting at Aberdeen, travelling up in the train from London. We rehearsed all the way. In Aberdeen I got a good notice. I rehearsed very badly and Shaw offered to teach me the part of Mrs. Linden but I don't think I wanted him to. (Ref E/Shaw letters). The Company was Janet Achurch, Charles Charrington, Courtenay Thorpe, Robert Farquharson and three others. We were the kind of company who took anything that our landlady would let us take from our rooms to decorate the stage for the performance – as we travelled very light.*

I had to have a typewriter in 'Candida' and my nightmare was that I should not be able to get one in the place we went to, as we were sometimes

only three days in one place. And I have undergone the ordeal of the Overture beginning and my sitting with no typewriter and had to open the scene typing and it was a very important prop – but it always did turn up but used to be every kind and sometimes wouldn't work (I really could not type) and one day when I pulled the papers out (the typewriter had been loaned in one of the University towns), when I pulled out the sheet it was all in Greek and I was so surprised that I nearly forgot my words. Another shock I got was that I found it was all written in red. As a result I used to get most awful nightmares. One of them was that Charrington said to me one night "I have not been able to get a typewriter but I have got a meat safe and a key and if you tap with the key it will sound like one" and he would pile up books all round so that it would not be seen from the front.

This was a fit-up tour and we went anywhere. In the Isle of Wight we played at Ryde. The theatre there had been leased by my grandfather for two seasons in the year and Mother and Aunt Kate played there. We used to go about in a wagonette and our stage clothes were all in one hamper. After playing at some tiny fit-up place we suddenly found ourselves at the principle theatre in Brighton with a huge stage. Our props seemed miles apart and we had to begin walking off much earlier to get to an exit as some of the stages were so small that we got off in one step.

Shaw wrote to me and asked me what I did in the way of business in the last act of 'Candida' because it had got such a good notice and he wanted to put it in as business in the printed copy.

Sometimes we acted on the end of piers and there was no booking beforehand. I remember on one occasion there were only about five people and they only came in because it came on to rain!

MRS BROWN-POTTER
1898 My Tour with Mrs. Brown-Potter in 'Charlotte Corday'

I had known Mrs. Brown-Potter and her sister in America and still used

*to go to see her in London. One day she sent for me and asked me if I would go on tour with her in 'Charlotte Corday' to play the part of —
——— (blank in manuscript) I accepted and we had quite a nice tour of No. 1 and No 2 towns (I remember being photographed in Glasgow at Annans).*

One thing always stays in my mind; a girl who played the ingenue part was put in my charge as she had never had any experience of life in the theatre before. She was quite good and had a personality that suited the part. We lodged together . There is quite an interesting story concerning this girl. Her father had been a wealthy man but had lost his money but went on living at the same rate as he had before, with no idea of cutting down expenses. The girl, who was with me, got sick of all the borrowing and said that she was going away to work for her living. She went to Charles Wyndham whom she had once met at a dinner and asked him if he would give her a part. She recited to him in rather a quavery and chary manner and he gave her a letter to some manager who didn't do anything. She was looking at the photographs of the London production of 'Charlotte Corday' taken in the vestibule of the theatre, when the manager came out and saw her and said "You have been sent for the part of the ingénue?" and she with great presence of mind said "Yes", and that is the way she came into the company.

I had never come across a girl who had never had anything to do with the theatre before and was in the company. Her attitude from the audience point of view, amazed me. She said "Of course I have been to the theatre a lot but I very often did not know the name of the play or the names of any of the actors – as a rule we used to come in after dinner, and very often we were late for the beginning and though we had programmes, we didn't trouble to read them." She belonged to the same period as a young man who said to Charles Hawtrey after seeing him in a play "I think it's marvellous of you to think of such funny things to say!"

CHAPTER TEN

Travels with my Mother

1893-4 HOLIDAY CANADA/AMERICA

EDY   *One year, instead of having a tour after the season at the Lyceum was*
finished, we went straight to America and took our holiday there. I think
we arrived early in September – we, i.e. Mother, Henry, Loveday
(Henry's stage manager) myself and of course, the two dressers Sally
Holland and Walter. We went straight to Montreal from Liverpool. We
went on a small boat because it was a longer voyage. I do not think that
there were more than half a dozen passengers except a community of
nuns. They used to sit in a tight little bunch on deck and say their offices.
They were going out to found a new house. I do not know whether they
were English or French nuns. They seemed to wear chiefly black and
rather unimpressive clothes – and off Newfoundland we struck the worst
fog that I have ever been in. We took ten days on that crossing and the
Captain was in an awful stew about it, saying we would be so late but
as we were on holiday, we did not care. Finally I got the impression that
he did not know where he was. The mouth of the St. Lawrence River is
difficult to negotiate and the sand or gravel used to silt up so that a man
used to go every day and put branches up to show where there were
banks. The hooter was going all day and all night on our ship and when
morning came the fog had lifted and we found ourselves quietly alongside
at Quebec, which is on the side of a hill and ramshackle, we thought. We
landed and went to have a look at the town and went up to see the Fort
where we got a lovely view of the St. Lawrence. The roads were fine and
the houses of wood. We saw and did Quebec in the little time we were

allowed. It was a lovely place and I should like to go there again. We then went back to the boat; we then went up the river, the course being marked by fir branches and then we arrived at Montreal. In this place there was nothing ramshackle to the general view although it is English, the French and America are very much to the fore.

No one knows what a maple tree is like until they have seen them. The whole scene seemed like one blazing scarlet forest. From there we took the train, our object being to travel to San Francisco by slow stages where the rest of the company were to meet us. We went first of all to one of the smaller of the big lakes, (the big ones being on the American side) where we got on to a lake steamer. I think it had paddles and inside there was a long room with a table down the middle where we had meals and the cabin doors opened on to it. The light came through the hatches above our heads. One day I was sitting there and it suddenly became dark and I thought it was a storm and the fog horn began. We were in the middle of a forest fire. We were all very excited and rushed up on deck to see it. We could see the flames through the smoke. The wood smoke made your eyes smart very much and as it cleared off, you could see rows of animals by the edge of the water, driven by fire – all kinds of animals who, in the ordinary way would have been enemies, were gathered together in peace owing to their common fear.

When we got through the lakes – we got on to our own train again and then stayed for the rest of the journey. It was Carnegie's own private train. We got on at Winnipeg. We travelled in the greatest comfort and luxury – in fact – perfection. The train consisted of an observation car at the end with a very roomy bedroom for my mother next to it. Then came a long sitting and a dining room with two pull-down beds in each. Loveday had one. Then Henry had a compartment (not such a nice one as Mother's!). I had one. Then came the kitchen and larder. This suite of Carnegie's was hooked on to any train and the cooks and assistants on our part belonged to Carnegie. The only snag was that the whole train was temperance and this did not suit the gentlemen of our party. At no station could we get a drink. The Canadian Pacific Railway was all temperate as the directors would not have it otherwise. Little bottles of something stronger than lemonade used to be brought in and put in the icebox. The cook and his assistants were French negroes and their cooking was perfection and our meals were a landmark in the day.

When you saw a maple tree you would see a scar down the trunk and a tin can tied round to catch the syrup. In some parts of Canada, the east, every now and again you saw a cultivated bit in the centre of which was the dwelling of a religious community. You never saw green grass, it was sort of yellowy and full of grasshoppers and insects. Then you came to the great corn belt. The furrows used to go for hundreds of miles and you saw nothing else. The earth is nearly black and very very rich. When they were ploughing, every now and then there was a shack and a railway station. At these stations we used to take on eggs and milk etc. At one of these little railway shacks, we smelt a lovely smell of scones being baked. Mother and I got out and went into the shack. We found a Scotswoman baking her scones and of course Mother fell on them and the woman was delighted to see us and gave us a very good tea. We were taking up water and that was the reason we had filled up. Until we got to Calgary, I don't think we stopped anywhere – and then we went into a siding and were met by an Englishman who had a ranch nearby which we drove to and stayed at for about four to five days.

In those days Calgary was only just a little bit of a place for disruption of journey. On this ranch they were growing hops. The hops there grow to a tremendous size. They were being picked by North American Indians. They looked so funny after being accustomed to see the Kentish hops being picked. Afterwards when I was in Cincinnati, I was going over one of the breweries, they showed me these enormous hops and I said how much bigger and finer they were than the English hops and they said they were not nearly so pungent as the English hops. They then brought in a handful of English hops and the smell of them pervaded the whole place. They told me they always put in a handful of English ones in every brew for the flavour.

In going to the Englishman's ranch we had to ride on a buckboard as there were no motorcars in those days. From there we went out to a picnic in the woods and Mother, who always had to have her afternoon sleep, took a hammock and hung it up and her hammock broke and she fell into the undergrowth, but she didn't mind and just slept on the ground. And when we had to start to go home, she was covered in mosquito bites so that you could hardly see what her face was! The men fared better because they had been smoking. I had been by the side of the water most of the time, watching the little chipmunks and the brown ermines running about.

When we were going over the Rockies, we went up and up and up, getting slower and slower, crawling round corners on a ledge in the rock. Snow all round and we had just come out of excessive heat. I asked the engine driver why we went so slowly (in a vague sort of way I thought it was to look at the view). He said it was the extreme danger – no one really realised it! Of course we went down on the other side just as slowly and when we got lower I thought I could see apple orchards, but when we got nearer, we saw they were peach orchards and all the little peach-fed hens running about in them. We passed through these orchards all day.

Vancouver
There we stayed a day or two, strolling about. This place was so different. We went into beautiful houses and talked to people we never saw afterwards. We were taken out driving in the park in a carriage and pair. Everyone was very nice. We had been away almost three weeks on the train – right away from people, only stopping at about half a dozen places on the way when we had stayed a night at hotels, but here we were taken right into the homes of the people who were more than kind.

In one place in the Rockies when we were in a siding, some people had thrown melon rind and other refuse and there were swarms of rats. I remember I was in the carriage alone when I saw them.

In the Rockies, I think it was Lake Louise, the lake was marvellous colours blues and greens and was a great depth but you could see down, it seemed like miles. They said it was very dangerous being between such huge mountains – great storms used to sweep down on it. In the Rockies at Glacier we went out riding – Mother – Henry, Loveday and myself just in our ordinary travelling clothes. On this ride our horses took the pace that Sir Henry rode, which was walking sedately.

I arranged to go out the next morning early, so off I went with the cowboys. How I didn't break the back of the horse I don't know because I went bump! bump! bump! The cowboy was doing the usual stunt of picking flowers from the saddle. When I got back to the hotel, I said to Mother "I feel rather stiff" and she said "You had better have a bath and keep moving about!" – cheery advice – until she found I had been riding in my alpaca skirt which is like a nutmeg grater and had no skin left to sit on! (I was very thin at that time)

Bit by bit we got to San Francisco where we went to the hotel where the company were to meet us next day and Henry started sending telegrams to know where they were and when they were going to arrive. We were not going to open for another week but he thought that we ought to be rehearsing for a week, the play being 'Henry VIII' with a lot of dances, music and supers to be rehearsed. The first telegram in answer to his was that there had been trouble with the staff and there would be delay. This was on account of the laws to do with labour (we travelled with our own electrician, stage carpenter, in fact we had about a dozen stagehands altogether). Henry got very worried but was very quiet and used to walk up and down at the quay when the boat was expected. Then he got a wire to say that two of the men who were in the cast had got lost at the World's Fair. Finally they all arrived the day before we opened. I went down with Henry to meet the boat and we walked up and down, up and down, up and down and oh! it was awful – he had had a whole week of holding himself in. Then we got to the theatre and pandemonium started. We started rehearsing the crowds, men hammering, scenery being shifted, ropes descending on your head, music being rehearsed, and that went on without a stop until we opened the following night when we gave the show. I was in the dance and had to dance with a perfectly strange person, who I had to pull through. We always had college boys as supers and it was here that I met Knoblauch. I consider that I got my best stage training in times like that.

'Dracula' published 1897
Bram Stoker wrote 'Dracula', or anyway had the proofs to correct, on our way out or return from America. He used to come to my cabin and read me bits of it, to get an idea of its effect on the general public. I was a very bad sailor and could not leave my cabin and so it was very convenient for him to bring down all his sheets and fix a passive resister with his eagle eye – as I couldn't help myself. The first part was all thrilling and exciting enough and helped to take my mind off my aches and pains. The bit he gloated about was the part when the lunatic caught flies on the windowpane and ate them. He explained the whole theory of it and made me sicker and sicker. I think after that he had to give it up and I don't think I remember much of the last part of 'Dracula'.

CHAPTER ELEVEN

Sarah and Lillie

31. Lillie Langtry and Sarah Bernhardt

In the late nineteenth century, Sarah Bernhardt and Lillie Langtry shared 'celebrity' status. Sarah was famous because she was truly a great actress of her time. Lillie had no such claim. Her beauty and her affairs gave her the notoriety she enjoyed and, as the mistress of the Prince of Wales, her decision to go on the stage and to set up her own management ensured her success. Edy knew them both, acted with them and worked for them. Her descriptions of her time spent with them gives us an unusual 'backstage' insight into their characters, seen by someone who was not only steeped in theatre but someone with a very discerning eye.

SARAH BERNHARDT

EDY   *I think I first met her at a supper at the Lyceum. The first thing I saw her act in was at Modjeska's Benefit 28 June 1881 Royal Princess's Theatre; she played a little romantic duologue called "Le Passant". She played a minstrel boy. I was thrilled by the entire evening. I was in a very high box and before the end I was nearly hanging out of it by my heels. Forbes Robertson was acting with Modjeska. Mother and Henry did something. Sarah was very gay, very young and very thin. I think it was her second visit to this country. After this I always used to go and see her in all the plays she did over here. Mother used to get a box. Then I used to go and sit in her dressing room. Everybody used to go round to her dressing room and many a time I have shared a seat on a dressing basket with Willie Clarkson whilst waiting to speak to her.*

CLARKSON'S   WIGS
are the most Artistic and Natural in the World.
Perruquier to the Leading Artists of the Day.
Amateur Performances attended on liberal terms.

CLARKSON'S   LILLIE   POWDER,
Used by Madame Adelina Patti, Mrs Langtry, Madame
Marie Roze, Mrs Kendal, Miss Fortescue, Madame Albani, Miss
Millward, Miss Violet Cameron, Miss Agnes Huntington, Miss
Phyllis Broughton, Miss Marie Tempest, Miss Julia Neilson,
&c. Price, 1s 6d. per Box. Per Post, 1s. 8d. W. CLARKSON,
THEATRICAL AND PRIVATE WIG MAKER, by Special
Appointment to Her Majesty the Queen, 45, WELLINGTON-
STREET. STRAND.

32. Copy of Advertisement for Lillie Powder

Willie Clarkson, the celebrated wig-maker and costumier, knew everyone in the theatre. He claimed his "Lillie Powder" was used by every famous actress of the day and his "Kleeno" was reputedly used by Henry Irving. The foundation stone for his new premises 41-43 Wardour Street (now a Chinese restaurant) was laid by Sarah Bernhardt in 1904.

Helena Modjeska (aka Helena Modrzejewska (1840-1909), was a renowned Polish actress who specialized in Shakespearean roles.

EDY   *One year when she came to Daly's theatre and was opening in 'Izaël', I heard they wanted supers and so applied in the ordinary way and got taken on and before Sarah arrived we were rehearsed by some Frenchman she sent over to get things right in the theatre. On the Sunday before we opened, I remember it well because it was a very hot day, we had rehearsed all morning and it came time for us to go out to lunch, and we all adjourned, but in those days there was nothing open. I remember sitting on a bench in Leicester Square and feeling very hungry. All the other supers were chorus girls and one of them came up to me and said "I am friends with the manager of the Leicester Lounge – come along with me and we will get something." So off we went and to my astonishment, I found myself in a sort of bar (I had never been in one before). The girl had a brandy and soda and when I was asked what I would have, I said "a lemonade" and we had biscuits – that was all we had all day. We didn't know that the rehearsal was going to last so long.*

In the evening, Sarah arrived – we had been rehearsing shouting crowds. Sarah came straight from the train to the theatre. We were all lined up and Sarah walked down the line as a Colonel reviewing troops. When she came to me, she just stopped for a moment with a twinkle in her eye and then passed on. Then we rehearsed the play and when all the others had gone, I hung behind and she said to me "What on earth are you doing this for?" So I said I wanted to see all the plays and see them close and so had joined as a super and was being paid. Sarah was very much amused. The first week was a hectic week – then came Friday payday – when we went to get it, it was *very much less than I expected. Several of the girls protested so I led a strike and most indignantly said that they paid £1 a week at the Lyceum and that if they did not pay that, that I would go straight to Madame Bernhardt. At first. …* would not give it, but on my threat of going to Madame Bernhardt – we received £1. We had all been working like blacks.*

*blank space in notebook

Sarah asked me to go with her to some exhibition at Olympia. She said, "I must go in the morning because I have lunch and after that I must drive in Richmond Park then go to have a fitting and then to the theatre and after that a supper engagement". So I went down to get her in the morning. She was staying at some place which looked over the park, the Hyde Park Hotel, I think. I went for her at ten, to find her still in bed, dictating letters to her secretary, arguing with her maid as to what she would wear in the day. There was some shop girl in the room waiting with shoes or hats, not knowing where or what she was, with French flying all around and this kind of pandemonium was going on.

Nothing seemed to stop but she got up, had her breakfast and put on a few clothes, had one of her long flowing garments put round her, screwed up her hair, jabbed on a hat and out we went, accompanied by the usual crowd, consisting of secretary and three or four other people. At Olympia, she hastened about, was very interested and animated – in fact not saving herself in the least – then we got back to her hotel for lunch, where she sat at the head of the table with an enormous white fur rug over her knees. (This rug always went about with her.) She always bought a new dog whenever she came to England – big dogs – and then she always used to take them back to France with her.

French musicians or artists used to drop in to lunch with her and she used to give the dogs large pieces from the table. Her dresser used to be at another little table with her hair all untidy. After this she would drive out to Richmond Park with coats, furs, shawls, rugs etc. I think she used to eat a little whilst the fitting (back at the hotel) was taking place and then down to the theatre where she gave, of course, a marvellous performance. (I being quite tired out.) If anything was not quite right, she would give half an hour's rehearsal after the show, then on to a supper party where she had kept everyone waiting. She had so much energy that she wore everyone else out. All her people, knowing what kind of a day they were going to have, if they got a moment, curled up and had a little sleep. Often have I been in and seen her dresser having one of these wee naps.

Sarah was very strict about the way people put their clothes on. All the principals wore theirs beautifully but she couldn't trust the supers and she had a kind of wardrobe man who used to stand at the foot of the stage, who used to have to to pass us and if he thought our hair was not well done or there was anything wrong with our dresses, we were sent up to put it right. Most of the walkers-on were short (on account of Sarah who was short – shorter than me) so most of the clothes were small. I had rather difficulty getting into mine especially in 'Tosca' in which I had to wear an Abbé's dress and I could not sit down in the scene at all. In one scene the supers used to have quite a good time, playing tiddlywinks on the gambling table until it was stopped. Unfortunately there were some people in a box who took a great interest in our game (this took place before Sarah came on) and our tiddlywinks was much more interesting than what was really going on in this scene – and we got hauled over the coals and were told not to do it any more. As a matter of fact, the people in the box were friends of mine.

I remember in 'Phèdre', she had a troop of maidens who trailed about after her in sort of white nightgowns with no sleeves and wreaths of pink roses on their heads. I was one of these horrors, and because I was the tallest, I came last and in the last act, when Sarah dies, she always had a girl on either side supporting the arms and I was put well to the back because I was too tall. One night she called to me and another woman who was with me (just before we went on) and made us walk on with her. This was alright until she came to dying when she flopped over on me (knowing that

33. Sarah Bernhardt in La Dame aux Camelias

whatever happened, I would not let her go) she put more and more weight on to me and it ended up my putting my knee into her back and flinging my arm over her – she was in fits of laughter and I was terrified.

(1890)
Another night, she said to me the night before "Put on an evening dress because I want you to go out with me after the show." She often did this. (I was 21 at the time because I remember putting on a dress that Mother had given to me for a birthday present. It was a yellow satin with buttercups.) She sent up her dresser and I came down in this dress (she was playing "La Dame Aux Camélias"). All we extras walked on in the gambling scene – and what was my horror and delight when she sent her dresser up to me at the beginning of the play to say "You are to go on with me in the first act". So on I went, shaking at the knees and was afraid of getting into the wrong place and wondering when I had to get off.

I was seated next to Sarah at the supper table and must have looked a most awful fish out of water at this courtesan's supper party. I must have looked most miserable and not at all right. I finally got off with prudence and then drew a long breath of relief. Sarah was always playing these sort of pranks.

On one occasion when Mother and I went to Paris for Holy Week, we went to see Sarah and had lunch with her – she ate a steak about two inches thick – it was the best steak I have ever had. As usual she sat in a beautiful high-backed chair with a white fur over her knees. A lot of people were at lunch. I never knew Sarah have a meal by herself. Then they started discussing an actress, who was playing a part in 'Cyrano' and saying how bad she was and Sarah kept saying "pas si mal, pas si mal." There was also a playwright who was writing a play for her and she did not like something about it and there was great discussion over this.

After lunch she took us into the garden and showed us the animals she had had given to her – they were in cages. There was a cheetah, a monkey and I can't remember what else.

Then she said she must go up and see her aunts before she drove Mother back to her hotel. It was one of those narrow tall houses, and after saying goodbye to all her different aunts, who all had some complaint and wanted her to get them this and that, and wanted to have their chocolate, one at this time and one at that, (she was keeping all kinds of vague relatives). They all seemed to have rather yellowy faces and wore little black chenille nets over their hair and mittens and little black aprons and always had complaints. Sarah, Mother and I then got into her carriage and drove off and out of every window a little chenille netted head was out of each window, waving a handkerchief in farewell.

'Fedora' – London
One day when she was playing 'Fedora' – there were no supers in this and I used to go down and watch from the side – at the end of one of the acts, Sarah had to dash up to the back of the stage, fling open double doors, see

104

the man on a bed, dying with all the doctors etc., standing round. It was a boxed in scene and I could not see very much. Maurice, Sarah's son had just arrived off the boat and he was very mischievous. He had a look at the scene and knew what it was about, rushed out to the back and got the man off the bed or couch and got there himself. Sarah had been acting a terrific scene and when the door opened, she saw it was Maurice, whom she thought was in Paris. Of course she was delighted after the scene was over – but she kept saying "méchant, méchant". This was at Daly's Theatre.

Rumour has it that the Prince of Wales (later King Edward VII) also surprised her by playing the part of the dying man on the bed. It is interesting to note that he had a strong penchant for famous actresses, as it is reputed that he was lover to both Sarah Bernhardt and Lillie Langtry – amongst others.

34. Lillie Langtry, British actress, 1901.

EDY

LILLIE LANGTRY

I met her first with Mother. She didn't like me at all but liked Teddy and was always asking Mother "Where is that lovely boy of yours?"

This was before Mrs. L was on the stage and when she was the reigning beauty. She used to get Teddy to go and sit by her. He was quite young and used to blush and be rather shy – but all the same he rather liked it. She used to take no notice of me.

I did not really think she was very beautiful. My idea being golden curls, pink cheeks and rather made-up eyes (my taste was meretricious in those days). Her eyes were perfectly beautiful – they were a beautiful grey and they used to go dark – but they were the kind of eye you could look into – not thick, translucent. I liked her.

1890

Then we did not see her for a long time. The next time I saw her she was playing Rosalind and she had certain qualities that came in very well – her appearance was very good and she didn't frisk about too much. It was a beautiful production. It was the second time I had seen the play and it was one I liked very much. Teddy and I used to act it when we were children.

1901/2 After that I saw her in several society plays – 'Peril' was one – she always wore very nice clothes – she had very good taste. Later on she built the Imperial Theatre and opened it with 'The Queen's Necklace'. In it Robert Tabor was acting and he asked Mrs. Langtry if he could have his dress made by me (by this time I had started my costume shop). Mrs. L. said "Yes". It was a great success (and a very difficult dress to make) she was pleased with the result and it was cheap. Later on when she did the play 'Mademoiselle Mars', I had the making of all the clothes and I worked in the theatre. I then got to know her as a worker. She was the first into the theatre and the last to leave it. I could always get on with a worker.

She had a maid, a dresser and a secretary all of whom used to shake in

35.Lillie Langtry as Lady Ormonde in *Peril*

their shoes and used to say to me "Oh don't speak to her today" and I used to say "I must see her" and I think she used to swipe [sic] the floor with them and she used to have fearful attacks of rage, but very often it was because they were very stupid and she would not stand a mistake. I wasn't afraid of her and didn't mind if she got into a rage, if there was cause and I was very much in sympathy with her.

I worked out the schemes for all the clothes with my old bodices and she used sometimes to say she wanted this or that (I made a dress of which I had shown her the design and which she had passed) this was for Miss Madge MacIntosh and was a little green coat and a long white skirt which she wore most beautifully. She was a rival actress in the play. Mrs. L. had had her clothes made in Paris and Lewis Walter played Napoleon and their dresses had been made irrespective of expense.

When Mrs. Langtry saw the dress at dress rehearsal she said it wouldn't do and the dresser, maid etc all shook in their shoes and said "Now you've done it!" It took all my tact to assure her that this dress was such a contrast to hers, that it would show hers up to advantage, that at length she accepted it. The real reason for her not liking Miss MacIntosh's dress was of course that she looked so much better than Mrs. Langtry!

On one occasion I was in her dressing room and she said to someone who was present "There, I can work with her. I asked her one morning for 27 more uniforms and in the evening they were there". This was not so marvellous as I already had the uniforms, but I always went on the tack of never saying anything was impossible.

During the run of the play, her daughter came back from school and was launched in society – she was dark and a beautiful girl and devoted to her mother. Then we had a busy time up in the wardrobe. The play ran for some time and there were always jobs there and I had a small staff. But for me it was not a whole time job. But now Miss Langtry had to have a different frock every evening and there was not too much money, so one frock had to be made into several different ones. In those days there were more frills and feathers, so it was easier to alter them than it would have been with the present-day dress. (I was doing this work).
1901 Miss. L. then got engaged and there was great excitement at the theatre and everyone was thrilled!

Jeanne Langtry married Ian Malcolm in 1902.

EDY   *One day Mrs. L was looking very depressed and I said, "What's the matter?" and she said "She's done the right thing. I know she's done the right thing but oh, I wish she had run off with any one she really cared for".*

Of course she was run after by semi-royalties etc. Mrs. Langtry had nothing to do with the marriage. Her daughter was under the wing of some high society women who arranged everything. Mrs. Langtry went off to Jersey where the wedding took place. She asked me to go with her and I have always regretted that I didn't. She was very unhappy. Although she was not a very good actress, she adored the theatre, as if she had not, she could not have lived in it and worked in it as she did.

She had a little house – the smallest in London I think. It was just by Madame Tussaud's and the back opened on to Regents Park. She also lived in Monte Carlo. She was always very generous but she did not get on too well with her fellow actors in the theatre. She had not good taste in her house. She had lots of beautiful things but some very tawdry things mixed up with them.

CHAPTER TWELVE

"In Paris, Everybody Wants to be an Actor Nobody Wants to be a Spectator"

– Jean Cocteau

EDY

Mother and I often used to go out to Paris for Holy Week. Sometimes Teddy or other friends of my mother went also. On one occasion Mother came to the little hotel where I was staying – she usually went to a smarter one – but on this occasion I had persuaded her to come to the one at which I was staying – The Oxford and Cambridge in the Rue d'Algiers. Mother had been out buying a lot of things and had sent them to the hotel to be paid for. Then she had gone on to the Bank to get some money and through some complication, she could not get the money. The result was that, Mother almost weeping, the Bank saying that they would have to wait until they heard from London, as, though she swore to her identity, they would not take her word. I then suggested that we should go and get Sarah or Coquelin or someone who would vouch for her. She was almost in tears by this time. In the meantime we went round to the hotel which was quite a modest little place, where Mother said as we went in "Pay the fiacre!" to the manageress who was at the desk in the office. The proprietress called me on one side and said "a lot of parcels arrived but as they were not paid for, I sent them back" and I explained that we had not any money at the moment and would be glad if they would pay. Madame called Monsieur who said that if they had been my parcels they would pay (I had been there for some time – Mother had

only just arrived) but then they said "We do not know this other lady!"
I said "We are going to see Madame Sarah Bernhardt and Monsieur Coquelin."
They said "Do you know them?" and we said "Yes".
Then I said "My mother is an actress and played in Shakespeare – Portia, Beatrice, Ophelia, etc."
They exclaimed "Oh, Shakespeare! Of course we will pay! Why didn't you tell us before that Madame played in Shakespeare?!!"

COQUELIN 1841-1909

One of France's greatest actors, was known as Coquelin the Elder, who acted and toured America with Sarah Bernhardt. His most famous role was Cyrano de Bergerac with Sarah Bernhardt playing Roxanne.

36. Coquelin as Cyrano de Bergerac

EDY   *The first time I ever saw him he came to the Lyceum to supper and he and H.I. both played the play called 'The Polish Jew' in French and 'The Bells' in English. Their conception of the part was totally different, and when you saw these two men together and were familiar with their method of acting, you realized that it couldn't be otherwise. Coquelin's idea was of a cold-blooded murderer with no conscience at all. Henry's was a man, eventually killed by the workings of his conscience. I never quite knew how Coquelin accounted for the imagination of the bells which were not there, or for the effect of the dream about the mesmerist, could have killed him.*

Coquelin's dresser
He had a dresser who had been an English groom, who used to make his noses for him and used to keep them in a cocoa tin. Sometimes he had to change noses as if he knocked against anything, it upset the contour. Coquelin gave me one of those noses as a memento. The last time I saw him he was playing Cyrano and Sarah Bernhardt was playing Roxanne at His Majesty's.
1897
When we went to Paris this time we went to see 'Cyrano de Bergerac' Mother wrote to Henry to tell him that it would suit him. He then gave me money to stay on in Paris and I went to the little hotel Oxford and Cambridge as it was cheaper and I was thus able to stay in Paris for longer. I was making a prompt copy of 'Cyrano' for Henry. Richard Harding Davis was staying in Paris at the time. He was waiting there for news from America and he was kicking up his heels not having anything to do. So, as I had not anything to do in the day, he used to take me out to all kinds of exciting places. We went to all the ordinary places where tourists go, and to places I remember very well.

Richard Harding Davis (1864-1916) was a popular writer of fiction and drama, and a journalist famous for his coverage of the Spanish-American War, the Second Boer War and the First World War.

37. Aristide Bruant by Toulouse-Lautrec

EDY   *One was a café run by Bruant. I think he was a Tundens* [sic] *Red*? –*
he used to wear a red shirt and top boots and sing revolutionary songs.
One night he stood up on the back of my chair when he sang and Dick
Davis asked me if I was afraid. I said no – of course I was enjoying it. I
had a revolutionary magazine which he gave me and signed.

* I have failed to understand the reference to *Tundens Red*, which may or may
not be due to Jacko's spelling or misinterpretation.

Aristide Bruant was not a "revolutionary" in the political sense but a highly popular
ballad-writer who performed in Montmartre in his own little café, La Mirliton at
84 Boulevard Rochechouart, the former site of Le Chat Noir, another popular

cabaret café that had moved to larger premises. At La Mirliton, Bruant greeted his clients in a very robust and unusual familiar way, sometimes calling them 'pigs'.

I can do no better than quote Eliot Gregory, American writer of the time who saw him in action and sets the scene perfectly adding colour and background to Edy's description of the evening. Her French and that of her companion obviously did not extend to understanding the lyrics and she may have thought she was listening to revolutionary propaganda when in fact, Bruant was telling the stories of "the poor and humble".

Eliot Gregory writes:-
"To give an account of the "Mirliton" is to tell the story of Bruant, the most popular ballad-writer in France to-day. This original and eccentric poet is as well-known to a Parisian as the boulevards or the Arc de Triomphe. His costume of shabby black velvet, Brittany waistcoat, red shirt, top-boots, and enormous hat is a familiar feature in the caricatures and prints of the day. His little *cabaret* remains closed during the day, opening its doors toward evening. The personality of the ballad-writer pervades the atmosphere. He walks about the tiny place hailing his acquaintances with some gay epigram, receiving strangers with easy familiarity or chilling disdain, as the humor takes him; then in a moment, with a rapid change of expression, pouring out the ringing lines of one of his ballads – always the story of the poor and humble, for he has identified himself with the outcast and the disinherited."

In 1892 Bruant was honoured as member of the society of *Gens de Lettres*. The French poet and novelist Francois Coppée said on that occasion "He has sought his inspiration in the gutter, it is true, but he has seen there a reflection of the stars."

EDY   *Another place we went had been one of the palaces of one of the Cardinals. It had now become a sort of doss house. It had big wooden tables with people sitting eating and drinking at them (very rough food) and some people lying sleeping on the floor. The house was beautiful and you could see little bits of marble inlay. I believe it was called "La Maison Rouge". There were awful scribbles and drawings on the walls.*

Then we also used to go to some very good restaurants for food which he knew of. Ethel Barrymore came over from London for a weekend. Dick Davis was very much in love with her and she wouldn't do anything that he wanted. He was not too well-tempered and they had an awful row and Dick Davis flew into a rage and a plate was smashed and Ethel Barrymore returned to London. After that Dick spent his time pouring out his woes to me and said I was most sympathetic. I was really busy eating my lunch. Talk, talk, talk until we were moved out of the restaurant because it was time for the next meal and then we moved on to another restaurant.

Some friends of his were passing through Paris and he wanted to give them a meal at a certain restaurant where they had very good food but which was not too respectable – as they were American girls he wanted a chaperone so he made me act as chaperone and named me Lady Henry Foster and they called me Lady Henry all evening (one of them was the present Lady Astor). He had a private room and I chaperoned them all evening. Dick Davis was so pleased with the way I did it that he gave me a gold purse the next day.

(Duplicate description in the notebook)
1897 I went over with my Mother to see the first night of 'Cyrano de Bergerac' in Paris and Mother wired to Henry or Henry wired for the rights of the translation. I was told to stay behind and make a prompt copy of the action of the play. Henry gave me enough money to live on at a little hotel in the Rue d'Algiers for a fortnight. I had the run of the theatre at the back and used to go behind the scenes and I managed to stay on in Paris on the same money for six weeks by going to very very cheap restaurants which I found better than some of the others and bicycling everywhere. Also an American friend (Harding Davis) turned up who treated me to many a dinner while I listened sympathetically to his love affairs to a woman who was a friend of mine. Sometimes these conversations after lunch used to last until dinner time. I knew it was no good so tried to put him off as much as I could. When I met him

later in London he was enthusiastic about someone else so that was alright.)

Harding Davis was not the only one to be "enthusiastic about someone else". 1897 and 1898 were ominous years for Ellen Terry and Henry Irving, both on and off stage. Irving had an accident which damaged his knee and was unable to act for over a month. *Richard III* was withdrawn. The Lyceum Theatre's eighteenth season ended with a loss of £10,000. Much to Irving's annoyance, Ellen was now corresponding daily with George Bernard Shaw, who was urging her to distance herself from Irving who, he stated, was "unworthy of my Ellen". With the cancellation of *Richard III*, Ted was left without work and began to feel a failure. Ellen was worrying about her eyesight and the lacklustre parts that Irving was giving her. She was also aware that Irving was seeing a certain Mrs. Aria.

For Edy something momentous was about to happen. Ellen set up her own independent tour of the London suburbs. Edy went with her.

Enter Christopher St. John on a bicycle.

EDY   *1897/98 E.T.'S TOUR OF THE LONDON SUBURBS
        I MEET CHRISTOPHER ST. JOHN*
        Lyceum 1897
        'Olivia' 'Othello' 'Sans Gene' 'The Lady of Lyons'

        Henry Irving was still doing things at the Lyceum but without her.
        [Ellen Terry] *I acted Emilia in 'Othello', Sophie in 'Olivia', one of the princesses in 'Sans Gene'. I designed the dresses.*

Godwin's artistic influence on Ellen, Edy and Edward (Teddy) Gordon Craig was always apparent. Great painters were among their close friends, both in Europe and the United States. Ellen sat for many of the famous portrait painters of the time including her first husband, G.F. Watts, John Singer Sargent, Sir Johnston Forbes-Robertson, James Ferrier Pryde, Walford Graham Robertson and Cyril

Roberts. Her friends included Whistler, the American artist Joe Evans and the pre-Raphaelite painter Sir Edward Coley Burne-Jones.

1898
EDWARD BURNE-JONES

38. Love Among the Ruins, by Edward Burne-Jones

EDY   *Mother and myself went out on a very foggy road (Mother always used to like going out in such weather). He lived somewhere near Olympia, I think the house was called "The Grove". When we arrived he was painting by candlelight. We went in and he talked to us so nicely, but we knew that he was dying for us to go and so we did not stay long and left him with the candle a few inches from his canvas as you could only see dimly in the studio. His daughter was going to have a baby and Mother had just been given a parrot and she said "I must call my parrot the same name as your grandchild" and he said "We do not know if it will be a girl or a boy". So instead of writing to say Margaret had had a little girl, he sent a wire to say "Your parrot's name is Angela!".*

            I was in 'Pelleas and Melissande' as one of the women at the Prince of

Wales theatre. Forbes Robertson, Mrs. Patrick Campbell and I think Martin Harvey were in the cast. Just as I came in to the theatre one night, I saw the posters "Death of Burne-Jones" (1898). I was very sorry.

At the New Gallery at the Private View which was always a great treat. The pictures which were the fashion – were those of Abbey, Burne-Jones, Boughton, Pevsner, Tadema, Rosetti, Watts and if you were very modern – Sargent.

Friday 10 March 1899
MISS ELLEN TERRY
NARROWLY ESCAPES DEATH.
Miss Ellen Terry (Miss E. A. Wardell)
while acting the character of Portia in
the Merchant of Venice, at Fulham
Theatre, had a narrow escape from death.
Owing to an accident to the machinery the heavy roller of the curtain suddenly
fell, narrowly missing the lady's head.

EDY   *It was during this tour that I met Christopher St John.*

We were playing 'Olivia'. She came to the Grand Theatre at Fulham. She came to the theatre on a bicycle and wore a red coat and wore a small three-cornered hat. She came behind for the evening. Mother said "This girl does not know anything about the theatre, so look after her." I was mending a mitten at the time and promptly pricked her with it as I shook hands. I stuck on to her – thinking it rather a nuisance. After the play she rode her bicycle by the wheel of Mother's carriage and I thought she would be under it every minute. She had asked me during the evening to go and have lunch with her the next day. I think she lived at Whitehall Court in a huge room which overlooked the Thames. She was writing and used to do so at night. I think we were rehearsing for 'Robespierre' at the Lyceum at this time and Mother and I had rooms at the Howard Hotel, Norfolk Street to be near the Lyceum. Christopher used often to come to see us. I had by this time got a workroom at the corner of Great College Street –

Sally Fairchild had these rooms before and I took them when she left (just the ground floor). The house belonged to the Hon. Maud Stanley. It was at this house that I had my first workroom.

When Mother went to America, I went to live there. I got a lot of work designing and making clothes for the theatre. At that time I employed about six workers. When Mother went to America, Fred Terry and Julia Nielsen played 'Sweet Nell of Old Drury' for which I designed and made the costumes.

39. Fred Terry and his wife Julia Nielsen in *Sweet Nell of Old Drury*

I was then living at Kingston Vale and Christopher came to live with me, but she still kept her room. As I was working at the Haymarket for Fred and Julia, I had given up my workroom and would go in from Mother's summer cottage at Kingston Vale.

CHAPTER THIRTEEN

People I Knew

FRED ARCHER 1857 –1886 Champion Jockey

EDY   *I thought he was wonderful – he gave Mother a dog and I thought he knew everything about dogs and used to swank about him at school. I always used to swank like anything about anyone like that at school.*

In 1885 he rode 246 winners, a record that remained unbroken until Gordon Richards' 1933 season. Archer won the Epsom Derby five times and won a total of 21 classic races. An admirer of Ellen Terry, he gave her the terriers, Fussie and Drummie. Fussie became Sir Henry Irving's dog, a gift from Ellen.

JAMES BARRIE 1892-1904 Author

I met him after the first night of his first play 'Walker, London'. It was done at Toole's Theatre by Mr. Toole. Toole played the comic lad. Violet Vanbrugh and Seymour Hicks were also in the play. After the play we all went either under the stage or in Toole's dressing room to supper and Mother said "Who is that badly behaved little man?" who kept writing little notes to the lady who had been playing the lead and throwing them to her at the table. I shushed her and told her it was the author of the play. She didn't like it and though later she appeared to like him, she never got over this.

The lady receiving the notes was the actress Mary Ansell who, in 1891, had been recommended by Jerome K. Jerome for a substantial supporting role in Barrie's play *Walker, London*. The two became friends and she joined his family in caring for him when he fell very ill in 1893 and 1894. They married shortly after Barrie recovered, with her retiring from the stage, but the relationship was reportedly a sexless one and childless. In 1909 she had an affair with Gilbert Cannan (an associate of Barrie's in his anti-censorship activities) who at 25, was half her age, and when she refused to end it, Barrie granted her a divorce. This was highly unusual and stigmatised, and briefly became a social scandal.

The catalyst for this scandal was the explorer Robert Falcon Scott. He and Cannan had both been courting Kathleen Bruce. This lady decided to marry Scott, leaving Cannan disappointed and dejected. Mary Barrie felt so sorry for him that their relationship rapidly became an affair which culminated in Barrie divorcing Mary who then married Cannan. That marriage too ended in divorce and Cannan finished up in a mental institution.

EDY   *1904*

> *I did not see him again until he was doing 'Peter Pan' and he had come to the party that was always held by the George Lewis's every year on New Year's Eve. The party consisted of a gathering of the most brilliant people such as Oscar Wilde, Pinero, Comyns Carr etc. It was quite informal and after we had all drunk a good deal of punch, someone would rap upon the table and call upon someone to make a speech – on this occasion Barrie was called for but said "no!" The others, thinking he was being funny, cried "Come on – don't be silly!" and there was a lot of chaff – but he got sullen and sulky and sat back and quite spoilt the party – and that Mother couldn't stand.*

> *Barrie took the flat we had had at Adelphi Terrace, also the one above it which had belonged to Pennell. I had to go and see him to ask if 'The Old Lady shows her Medals' could be filmed with Mother as the Old Lady. This could not be done for some reason.*

> *He had a brick fireplace built with a wide hearth. On one side there was a sort of box which contained peat. On the other side was a box containing logs. On this wall there was a rack of dirty old papers. There*

was a mattress on the top of the boxes on which he slept covered by an old Jaeger blanket. There were curtains which could be drawn which made a tiny little cubby hole, where, he told me, that when he was alone, he liked to be. This was in Pennell's flat which he had also taken and which was above the one that Christopher St. John and I had lived in.

LADY FLORENCE BELL 1851-1930 author, playwright

EDY *She was very kind – but if what she wanted to do was not kind, she did not care, and most people danced to her tune. She said what she approved of was working things with a committee of one and this she was able to do, and if she made a mistake she stood by it. This quality made other people work.*

At breakfast she came down in a black quilted dressing gown over her very tall thin figure, a priceless chinchilla cape over that and a piece of black lace over a piece of white lace tied firmly under her chin – and cotton gloves. She had a trolley on her right side full of papers and newspapers – on her other side she had an empty one on which she put all her letters that had to be answered and the papers and many magazines she had to read. A huge waste paper basket into which she threw all the letters that didn't want an answer and those she did not like. I think she had a pencil with which she made notes on her letters for her secretary to deal with later.

SIR SEFTON BRANCKER 1877-1930 Pioneer of British aviation

EDY *Used to fly quite low – he came over Priest's House. He used to say that he could see the house quite plainly. He came and spent the day with us and used to tell me about his servant, who was very devoted to him, and always used to say that he tried out things that he need not, and was always so afraid of him being picked out of a smash and he said they would know him by the eyeglass he always wore. As a matter of fact, when his body was discovered in the smash, it was found that he had several eyeglasses in his tunic pocket.*

October 4, 1930: Attempting to fly to India, British air minister Lord Thompson and civil aviation director Sir Sefton Brancker were killed when the airship R101 exploded after hitting a hillside after losing height in heavy rain near Beauvais, France. Only eight of the fifty-six people aboard survived the crash. The crash was caused by an overweight, underpowered airship caught in heavy rain.

ROBERT BROWNING 1812–1889 Poet

EDY

When I think of him, I remember his hearty laugh. At the time I knew him he had a neat white beard. I knew he was a poet and I had his works but I don't think I understood much about his poetry. In those days I was not at all keen on food, as children are as a rule, and I had great scorn for those who had – and particularly a poet. He was a gourmet and understood food to a nicety. We always met at the home of a Mrs. Skirrow. She was extremely fat and had eyes like a pig in a fat face. She had a marvelous cook. Her attractions, which didn't quite jump to the eye, were quite manifest at her table. I couldn't understand this. Probably she admired Browning very much. Anyone of any note could be found at her table. She was a most kind and hospitable person and I was always asked with Mother. I often wonder why I was asked to all these places with Mother, as people must have been awfully bored with me. As a good education though, being taken by Mother I came in contact with the most distinguished people – though I did not realise it at the time.

BURNAND F.C. 1880-1906

The Editor of Punch, we both loved. He had a lot of children and we used to play with them. We thought that being the Editor of Punch was absolutely it. We had always had Punch and he used to be perfectly darling to us. We had met the Editor of the "Daily Telegraph", who frightened us very much and I have never been able to read the Telegraph since, because he frightened me so much. In later years I used to go to dinner at the Burnand's and Mrs. Burnand was very nice to me. I always used to go as a shadow to Mother and used to look on at most of these outings.

MRS. BURNETT 1849-1924 Author (Frances Eliza Hodgson Burnett) *The Secret Garden, Little Lord Fauntleroy*
The Secret Garden is set in Yorkshire, at the fictional Misselthwaite Manor, but the garden at Great Maytham Hall, at Rolvenden, Kent, which Hodgson Burnett rented in 1898, was the inspiration.

EDY *1898*
She used to come and see us at Smallhythe and because she used to like it so much she built a cottage here. She lived at Great Maytham Hall at Rolvenden, where she had this lovely garden which was walled round by laurel. Inside were flowering shrubs. It was really an orchard, with old apple and pear trees which no longer had any apples and pears, but when they grew old enough, she used to grow climbing roses in profusion over the old trees. This is what really was her secret garden. She had a little table and a garden seat. She used to write there and the birds used to come and sit on the table and on the paper on which she was writing – they were so tame that they didn't even seem to mind when we were there.

1889 I remember going to see the dramatized version of 'Little Lord Fauntleroy'. Aunt Marion was "dearest" and little Vera Beringer played Little Lord Fauntleroy and when she had to be most loving to Marion, she used to be perfectly awful. If Marion said "Now you mustn't do this or that" she used to be perfectly awful and bite and kick Marion, who got to be perfectly terrified of her. Mrs. Burnett was a very nice kind woman and she always used to bring us plants and things which she was dividing up in her garden.

SIR ALFRED GILBERT, RA 1854-1934 Sculptor. Gilbert's best known work is the Eros in Piccadilly Circus.

EDY *Visit to Bruges*
Christopher, Mother, Pixie Colman Smith and I all went over.
We had written to the Panier d'Or for rooms which had been recommended to us. The place was packed and the only place that we

could get was over a baker's shop with four beds in one room. It also had four chairs and a tiny washstand. The floor was sanded and one small window. We didn't know how to get it dark (which Mother always wanted) without blocking out the air so we blocked it out and nearly died of heat. Every time the carillon sounded, Mother woke up and said "What's that?"

In the morning it was awful. Mother washed all over in a small basin and splashed the water all over the place. The others, some washed and others didn't. Mother wrote a note to Alfred Gilbert and we left it at the door. Then we went back and later Mother was getting up when a large bunch of roses arrived from him and an invitation to dinner. When we arrived at Bruges there was a huge procession going through the town. We were on the outskirts of the crowd so, as we were coming from the station by back ways, we could not see much. Suddenly we heard a blast of trumpets – the same trumpet calls that we had always used in Louis XI to announce the envoy. Imagine our surprise when we heard it in the procession. King Leopold was there with two little girls in starched frocks with blue sashes in a landau.

Alfred Gilbert came and fetched us in a carriage and told us that his wife was a bit touched and not to mention a certain thing as this always set her off. The conversation at dinner was the jerkiest as we were always having to pull ourselves up, being on the verge of using it. After that he asked us to a picnic in the forest and we went in the local omnibus. We on the outside to see the view, also three friends of his – and he went in the inside and said he didn't feel very well. He would not eat anything at the picnic. It was in a pine forest with the soft pine needles under foot. We took snapshots and amused ourselves generally. I had my first Kodak and was taking snapshots all the time. The Kodak was a new thing then. He used to be so very depressed and then suddenly so gay – he was always up and down – up and down.

He was working on the head of a woman who was sitting for it and of her dead husband from a photograph. She had curly hair and he seemed to have worked in little heads of cupids in the curls of her hair and round the base. At first you do not see them. It was only going up close to it that you saw it was cupids. It was really rather lovely. He used to make beautiful little pieces of jewellery and sell them in Bruxelles and told me that he still made enough money out of this for his cigarettes.

40. Eros in Piccadilly Circus by Gilbert

Before the Eros in Piccadilly was opened (1893) and was still under a sheet, we were coming home from the theatre (which he was very keen on – he often came to supper at the Lyceum), we went under the sheet. I couldn't see much of the Eros – only the dolphins' heads. He gave me a bit of the bronze which had chipped off them.

ACTORS I KNEW
EDWIN BOOTH 1833-1893 American Shakespearean actor, younger brother of John Wilkes Booth, who assassinated President Abraham Lincoln. Edwin Booth came to the Lyceum in London in 1881, alternating the parts of Othello

and Iago with Henry Irving. At the time his wife was seriously ill. Their daughter was with them and she had the responsibility of caring for her mother while Booth was performing. Edy says he had "really a lot to be sad about" but does not mention his wife's terminal illness.

EDY   *1881 I remember seeing Edwin Booth. He played the part of Othello. I do not think I thought he was very great. But he was very nice to me off the stage. He had a very luminous eye but to me he seemed to stand in the middle of the stage and shout. I never saw him as Iago, so never saw Henry Irving as Othello. Edwin Booth seemed very solemn – not like the other actors I had met, as even H.I. used to chuckle. Afterwards I knew that he had really a lot to be sad about as he had had a very bad season before he came to H.I. at the Lyceum.*

41. Edwin Booth as Iago

EDY   *I remember Mother saying "I shall have a nice easy night tonight because Booth is playing Othello." When Henry played it, she got black from top to toe as he was so violent. He never felt that he got the part the way he wanted. The last night he acted the part of Othello, when he came off after the last call, he threw his turban on the ground and said to Mother "That is the last time I shall ever play that part!"*

LUDWIG BARNAY 1842-1924 German actor
His father was an orthodox Jew who disapproved of his son's acting talents and who eventually disowned him. Barnay became a member of the Meiningen Court Company and was acclaimed for his performances in 'Hamlet', 'King Lear' and 'Julius Caesar'.

On the third tour of America by Henry Irving and Ellen Terry, there was a terrible blizzard, making it very difficult to get from their respective hotels to the theatre. Ellen noted that Ludwig Barnay was due "to open the same night in New York but the blizzard affected his nerves to such an extent that he did not appear at all, and returned to Germany directly the weather improved!"

42 Ludwig Barnay

EDY   *1881*

He came to the Lyceum Theatre and I met him there. I saw him first acting with the Duke of Saxe-Meiningen's company. He played in 'Julius Caesar' as Mark Anthony and it was the first time that any company had used their supers dramatically and pictorially and had them properly trained. In those days supers were just paid 1/-(one shilling) a night and just stood or went on when they were told and walk across when the supermaster told them to. But these people all played parts. Henry Irving and Beerbohm Tree modelled their supers on them afterwards.

When I went to study in Germany, he gave me the run of his theatre. I went to every play that I wanted to and saw many Shakespearian plays and also the play which the Kaiser had written. I often saw him going in. I saw many of the modern German plays and was very amused with them and liked them. One of the actresses who was in the national theatre and played a small part, used to give me lessons in German but I learnt much more by going to see the performances at the theatre.

He made my stay in Berlin very homely. He lived in a flat over the theatre and his wife and daughter were very kind to me and I used to go about a lot with his daughter. I used to go to see a rehearsal and then pop up and have lunch with them. I think that this is the best way to live when you are working in the theatre.

EMMA CALVÉ 1858-1942 French opera singer
One of the first divas, Calvé was very temperamental and intense.
She was described as having an "extraordinary" voice as can be heard on her recordings.

        1893

EDY   *The first time I heard Calvé sing was in her bath. It was during the year when New York was full of theatre and opera artists. We were staying at the Plaza Hotel and Calvé had the suite next to us. Whenever she had a bath she used to sing loudly. Mother was very fond of her and she often came in to talk to us. I remember her complaining about the rehearsals at the opera – at least the want of them – and after a great deal of bother, she prevailed upon De Reszke to go down to rehearse 'Carmen' and she was so furious because he would only hum and give her cues, as she was prepared to do it as it was to be done at night. She used to get very excited telling us all about it, saying "If I can do it, why can't he?"*

43. Calvé as Carmen

The Metropolitan Opera House and the Theatre we were in were under the same management (Abbey)*, so whenever I wasn't walking on or playing a two-line part in the H.I. production, I used to go round to the Opera House. It was a very magnificent building and held heaps of people and had a large stage. But I think it must have been rather old as, on one night when they were playing 'Carmen' and beautiful white horses came on in the last scene, something scared them and they plunged a bit, one of them going right through the stage and disappearing, creating quite a disturbance. Then there was a big dinner given to*

*Mother and Henry I think and we all went. We were all seated at the
table and Calvé had not appeared. She came in very late looking very
beautiful with scarves wrapped round her head. One of the prima
donnas said she "wanted to make an entrance".*

DAME NELLIE MELBA, GBE 1861-1931

Born in Australia, Nellie Melba not only enjoyed international renown as an
opera singer but also gave her name to Melba Toast and Peach Melba, created for
her by the chef Escoffier. Dame Nellie together with the actress, May Whitty
(mother of Margaret Webster, one of Edy's lesbian friends) were the first
performers to be created Dame in the Order of the British Empire.

EDY   *Melba was also of this company and I saw her in 'Pagliacci' in which she
        made a great success. She came round one day to see Mother and I think
        she was doing something for a charity. She asked Mother if she got a great
        many begging letters and Mother said "Yes". Melba said "I have just had
        one this morning from a man in Sing-Sing, saying he is very musical and
        asking me if I would send him a banjo." Mother said "And are you doing
        so?" She said 'Yes" – she was always very generous and when Mother was
        in Australia during the war (1914-1918) they used both to do a lot of
        little things for charities.*

FANNY STIRLING 1815-1895

Mrs. Stirling was the actress who originally created the part of Peg Woffington
in '*Masks and Faces*'. After a modest career, she gained a considerable reputation
when she played The Nurse in Irving's 1882 production of '*Romeo and Juliet*'.
This is when Edy met her and loved to chat with her about her early days in the
theatre. Three years later Mrs Stirling also played Martha in *Faust* at the
Lyceum.

EDY   *1882 'Romeo and Juliet' was a play I didn't like (in those days). I hated
        the balcony scene – I used to sit on the bottom of the steps looking up to
        the balcony with Mrs. Stirling and she used to tell me all about things
        when she was young.*

44. Ellen Terry as Juliet with Fanny Stirling in *Romeo & Juliet* 1882

LUCIEN GUITRY 1860-1925 French actor

Guitry had strong associations with Russia where he appeared at the French Theatre in St Petersburg. His son, Sacha named after the Tsar Alexander III, was born there. Guitry was a friend of Peter Ilyich Tchaikovsky and his brother Modest and encouraged the Russian composer to write his *Fantasia Overture to Hamlet*. In 1888 he wrote to the composer, who was then on a concert tour abroad:

"I have taken upon myself the task of acting as the Grand Duchess's spokesman and to ask you whether you might not be able, if push comes to shove, to pull off not an overture, but an entr'acte for Hamlet's pantomime scene – in short, an entr'acte between the Theatre Scene (the allegorical murder) and the great portrait scene in the Queen's bedchamber, where Hamlet kills Polonius and the Ghost appears? I am writing all this to you against my better instincts, as I am aware of the magnitude of what I am asking. To write and to compose while hopping from one train to another is extremely difficult. However, as I said: I am acting here merely as a spokesman. It would have to be performed in a gala production at the Mariinsky Theatre, conducted by Nápravník, in the third week of Lent, i.e. in two months' time".

EDY   *1895 I first saw Guitry acting with Sarah Bernhardt in 'La Princess Lointaine' in her own theatre where he and she and (Edouard) de Max were the principle people in Rostand's play. The next time I saw him was on the stage at Daly's Theatre when he was supporting Sarah in her season there. I supered with him in the play 'Izaël' in which he played Mahomet. He was very much bigger than many of the French actors – very tall – which gave him the appearance of looking down on the other actors. He was very calm and quiet and spoke very steadily which was a great contrast to the excitableness [sic] of the other actors. Later I saw him act with his son (Sasha Guitry) and future daughter-in-law Yvonne Printemps.*

YVETTE GUILBERT 1865-1944 French cabaret singer
A diseuse par excellence, her risqué lyrics and extraordinary delivery made her a favourite of Freud, Shaw and King Edward VII. She appeared in the first talkie movies, in one film with Sacha Guitry. She was awarded the Légion d'Honneur in 1932 as *The Ambassadress of French Song*.

45. Yvette Guilbert by Toulouse-Lautrec

EDY   *She couldn't bear England – she said it was always cold and raining. The first time I saw her, I saw her from the side. I think it must have been at some special matinée. Not understanding what she said, I was more taken up with her appearance. She had on a plain white frock folded across the front and long black gloves and her hair screwed up. She did not appear to have much make-up on and didn't seem to care what she looked like – nor did anyone else.*

Those who didn't understand the language laughed very loud as they thought it was something improper. It wasn't always – but you couldn't tell because she used to do hardly anything and we had been accustomed to people winking or making gestures etc., etc. But she used to stand very still and didn't move much except in 'La Glu', then she did a little movement, but in her subtle songs she moved hardly at all. When she began she was just a turn in the Music Hall and sang songs. Later on she became a diseuse. The music hall artists of that time had no voices and used to speak because they couldn't sing. Edna May was the first that I remember who first sang in musical comedy, as before that in pantomime and musical comedy, no one used to sing. They shouted and it was the personality that got it over. After Edna May, they got people who could sing and the others were called 'diseuses'.

When E.G. [sic.Y.G.?] came back to England later and was at the Little Theatre, I used often to go and talk to her. She was a very very kind person but she was always very much affected by the rain and dank weather and that was her experience of London. In later years she got more ample in figure and this suited her better and her personality always used to get it over – she also was more ample in movement.

CHAPTER FOURTEEN

Home at Last

46. Smallhythe Place

THE FARM – SMALLHYTHE 1900

EDY   *We had the cottage at Winchelsea where Mother had people who used to come to stay with her for weekends. The chief form of entertainment was taking them for drives in the neighbourhood.*

HENRY IRVING AND THE SHRIMPS
On one of the trips to Rye from Winchelsea, Henry bought some shrimps which were given to him in a paper bag, and on the way home, he was

holding them on his knee, he suddenly became conscious of his knee being very damp, which puzzled him very much until he explained it by saying "Poor things, they are frightened!", at which we all yelled unmercifully.

A chief drive in the neighbourhood was to go to Tenterden where there were shops. Bormans shop was already there – we stayed at The White Lion on our way down from London to Winchelsea.

In driving over we had to stop to pay at the tollgate at Smallhythe, and Mother and all of us used to walk up the hill to save the horses and Mother always used to say "I should like to have that house". Martin was the shepherd "looker". who used to live in the house and Mother used to talk to him and, about the third time, she was asked in to have tea and went into the big room (kitchen) where the kettle was boiled on an oil stove. They used condensed milk and strong Indian tea.

On one of these convivial meals, she once said to the man, "Now, if ever this place is to be sold, you must mind and let me know." She had said this in lots of houses all over the world. She always used to say she collected cottages. For years we still went passed [sic] on the way to Tenterden.

In Tenterden one time we saw the Clowes Marionnettes. They were in a tent on the recreation ground. It was fearfully dusty all over the town, just one or two people lounging outside a pub. Henry, seeing a dramatic performance advertised, said "When does the performance take place?" of a girl in charge who was dusting things. She replied at an hour in the evening, which made it too late for them to get back to Winchelsea for supper. Henry said "How much do you take when your house is full?" He was told the sum. The Clowes family had all come out by this time and recognized H.I. Then the gentleman stuck it on and replied £5.5.0 (five guineas) So Henry said, "I will pay you for a show if you will give it earlier." Then our party went to the White Lion and had luncheon (where Mother always used to go into the kitchen to see what was being cooked – Miss Masefield was the proprietor) after which we went and saw the Grand Marionnettes performance. I remember there was a great transformation scene at the end. The audience on this occasion were five of us and the coachman so we paid a guinea for our seats. On one occasion we saw 'Maria Martin'. Mr. Clowes always after their visit announced on his programmes "Under the patronage of Mr. Henry Irving and Miss Ellen Terry".

When Mother started her own management, she forgot about Tenterden with all the other things she had to think of. And when she was on tour, she received a letter from the Martins (Smallhythe) to say that the farm and whole of the property was to be sold by auction and, as she had asked them to let her know, they were doing so. So she sent a telegram to Henry Gibson, saying that she would like to have it and would go up to a certain sum. And the next time she heard anything about it, was to say that she had got it and for less than she had said. It was a bad day for a sale as it was pouring with rain. She still had the house at Winchelsea at which she still spent most of her spare time.

The farm was in awful repair. There were great holes in the walls where the sacks of wool had been leaning against, as it had been a store for wool. The Martins still lived in it (in the yellow room) and slept in the room above. The rest of the place had been used to store wool.

With the farm she got a great lot of land which she didn't know what to do with. The man who bid against her at the sale really wanted the land, so he bought the land from her and she kept the house and the field behind for nothing. She got very much laughed at for buying it. As she was on tour, she sent a distinguished architect down to see it and he said there was a stack to do. The plaster was all sticking out where the sacks of wool had been leaning against it and was full of all kinds of 'animals'. The wool had been kept as there had been a slump in wool – it was being kept for a better market.

When she heard there was so much to do, she sat back and left it and started out on another tour. At the end of two years, Martin wrote to say that water was coming in at the roof and other places, so she came over and said "Oh, this isn't near the sea" and didn't like it. I said to her "I think if you have this and that done to it, I think you will like it." So she got a builder called Nun from Tenterden to come and look at it and gave him the order to get it right. This took over a year. Meantime the Martins went to a little house over the road (now called Martin's) which had been left to him by an old lady and Mother rented a little cottage on this side of the road (Priest's House) only one half of the cottage was under repair and was in fairly good condition. The other half which was in a shocking state, was inhabited by some farm labourers.

The Martins went to live at what is now Priest's House, which Mother had taken. This half was quite sealed off from the other half. Afterwards they went to live at their own cottage on the other side of the road. Martin was in Priest's House while the Farm was being repaired. Afterwards they lived across the road.

Then after the Farm was put in order, she still did not go and live there. So I asked her if I could get a certain amount of furniture and go and live there for the summer. So she said "Yes". About this time she was moving her London house and she saw that there would probably be some furniture that I might have from London.

Christopher and I rode down from London on a very hot day on bicycles (I had on a bolero and skirt with braid on it). We were so pleased to ride down the last hill where we stopped and asked someone in the road where the key was. We were told it was up at the vicarage at the top of the hill. We were not at all pleased at the thought of having to go up that hill again. We saw some people stop at the church and found they were the vicarage people who happened to have the key in their bag, which they gave us.

The furniture was supposed to be down there but nothing was. All that was in the farm was a bureau and a cupboard, so Chris and I went to the White Lion in Tenterden for the night. The next day we bought a spoon, a ham and two camp beds. Then we came back to receive the furniture but it didn't come for three days so we slept at the farm. It was very hot and Chris was gazing up the road and I said "I don't think they'll come today" and I went round to the back where I saw in the middle of the marsh, a huge yellow pantechnicon! Stuck! The men had walked on and come to ask the way and we told them it was for us. They had been told there was an awful hill on whichever road they came by and were told that the only way without a hill would be the marsh. The nearest station was Appledore, Rye or Headcorn. So then everyone about the place was collected and went and pushed and pulled, and at last the pantechnicon was put along side – and we were very unpopular because there was no pub anywhere near. The furniture wasn't at all suitable as it was all the stuff that Mother didn't want from the London house. Anyway we got one room comfortably furnished (this was the Terry Room) then we asked Mother to come and spend the weekend and see what it was like and she liked it very much. But it was still some time before she really took to it. Then she got the chance of letting Tower Cottage Winchelsea to Marshall Hall and that summer she spent in the farm.

Sir Edward Marshall-Hall, KC, 1858–1927 was an English barrister who had a formidable reputation as an orator. He successfully defended many people accused of notorious murders and became known as "The Great Defender".

EDY   *SMITH SQUARE 1900*
        The house that I had rented at the corner of Gt. College Street was wanted, as they were building a lot to enlarge the Westminster School. So I had to look for another and took No. 7 Smith Square. Christopher St. John and I shared this house and let the drawing room floor to another woman who had lived in the house at Gt College Street. She was very keen on spiritual meetings and table rappings. The house was haunted. The house was composed of four floors. On each floor there

was a front room, a back room and a powder closet. The spiritualist had to leave because the spirits used such bad language and she left. When I went to see it, the back room on the ground floor instead of being used as a sitting room, was full of boxes, fishing rods, coats etc., and the powder closet was not used at all – but I noticed a smell of stale incense in it so thought the previous people must have been catholics and used it for a little chapel.

When we went to live in the house, Christopher had this room to do her writing in, but I found that she would come and write in any room except this one, which was especially hers. So I said "don't you like that room?" and she said "No, I can't settle to write there". So I gave her the one I had and went there myself and had my desk and book and pictures moved into it. But I found exactly the same thing, that I came and worked anywhere except in that room. Later on, Penelope Wheeler, who was playing in Mother's season at the Imperial, wanted a room so we let it to her as a bedroom. She got very ill and her husband came and said she could not sleep and could she have another room. I said there wasn't one except an attic but he said she would rather have that. I asked her what was wrong with the room and she said she always felt that someone came into the middle of the room and then fell down and that she could never get to sleep after this. After this Pamela Colman-Smith had the room and she used to see and hear all kind of things. Then Billy Harcourt-Williams came to stay and could not sleep there.

Then our houseboy had it and I asked him if he heard anything and he said he heard footsteps and a thud but didn't mind it and went to sleep again. When I was in my sitting room upstairs, I used to hear what I thought was the maid going up to bed. I used to call to her to post some letters before she did so, but found on several occasions that she had been in bed for over an hour and there was nothing to account for the footsteps. Two men came from Cambridge belonging to the Psychic Roundtable with cameras and sat up all night but didn't see anything.

All the property there had belonged to the monks of Westminster and in lots of the gardens there were old fig trees, much older than the houses. In a corner of our garden people said they had seen a monk digging, but I never saw him. The former tenant had tried to have this ghost laid and the smell of incense that I had noticed on my first visit was due to that.

CHAPTER FIFTEEN

Of Plays and Players

MORE FUN ON STAGE AND BACKSTAGE

EDY   *While I was at Smith Square, I had a flat of three workrooms in Henrietta Street and employed about fourteen women and took on making private clothes as well as theatrical costumes. I had a lot of old wardrobe mistresses – they were all over sixty and they could run up theatre dresses but were no good in chiffon, frills etc., so often there wasn't much for them to do as they were not suitable for making private clothes.*

47. Edith Craig in *The Dead Heart*

142

1899 Robespierre
I had all the crowds to dress and all the small parts – I was told by the management to use up all the clothes in the wardrobe, if they were the right period, before making new ones.

Sir Henry always had his clothes made by the very best people, but not in the theatre – I think it was Pool [sic] *At the dress parade, Sir Henry did not like the look of a lot of the dresses in the huge crowd in the last act. He pulled one man out and said "He looks alright – I would like them all to look like that", at which I smiled. He said "What are you grinning at?" I replied "That was one of your best dresses in 'The Dead Heart' which had come into the wardrobe – well-worn but beautifully made. In the same play I had a chance to experiment with ghost dresses with which Sir Henry was very pleased.*

SHOCK-HEADED PETER
December 1901– I made the clothes for 'Shock-Headed Peter', a children's play at the Garrick. I was asked if I would make the clothes all found for a certain figure (very cheap!) The first one who came to me at Smith Square to be measured, his head showed above the fanlight of the front door – he was so tall. I didn't make much over the clothes!

Mrs. Kate Bishop, who had played in pantomime with Mother, played the mother in 'Shock-Headed Peter' and her little girl, Marie Löhr played one of the children. This play was one of Nigel Playfair's earliest productions. I remember working on one of the costumes all Christmas Day in one of the dressing rooms and Mother bringing me my dinner in a basket.

MARIE LOHR 1890-1975 Actress
Marie Löhr's mother Kate had acted with Ellen Terry in Bristol. Marie was born in Australia and made her first appearance on stage in Melbourne aged three. They moved to London in 1900 and the next year Marie starred in *Shock-Headed Peter* at the Garrick Theatre at the age of ten.

EDY   *FORGET-ME-NOT 1903?* [sic]

In this play I had to play Kyrle Bellew's fiancée and I was considerably taller than he was. To get over this difficulty, I had to always be sitting in all the scenes I had with him, and often most difficult thing I found was dropping on to a sofa. In the play I had to receive two letters. One was a pencil scrawl from the doctor and the other a beautiful letter which I had to read aloud to music. During the letter Forget-me-not has to appear. One night the wrong letter was given to me and the music began and I had not learnt a word of the letter I had to read, so had to take it every word from the prompter as it was very important. It was one of the most awful things I had to do in my life.

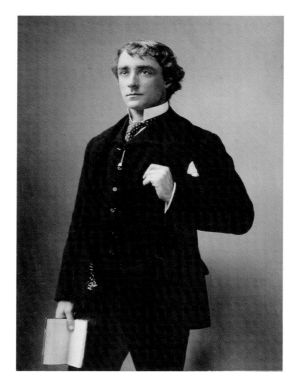

48. Kyrle Bellew

HAROLD KYRLE BELLEW (1855-1911), English actor

Everyone fell in love with Kyrle Bellew who was considered the handsomest man on the stage. He first appeared in Australia in 1874, but then joined Irving at the Lyceum from 1878 to 1880. In 1888 he joined Mrs. Brown-Potter on a tour round the world, and for the last ten years of his life played romantic and modern comedy parts in the United States where he died in Salt Lake City, Utah in 1911.

49.Ellen Terry as Hjordis in *The Vikings*

EDY   *THE VIKINGS April 15 1903*

When the production of 'The Vikings' came on, I made all the dresses which Teddy (Gordon Craig) *had designed. Mother had taken the Imperial Theatre and my brother did the entire production.*

The first thing I was given to make was a circular cloak consisting of different coloured squares in a special rotation. After having tried to lay the squares on the floor in every possible direction, I found that it was a well-known fact that what I had been asked to do was a scientific impossibility. My brother said "Oh, if you can't make them, I can get them done at Hampstead!" When the cloaks appeared from there, they were quite different from the drawings and directions I had been given and not circular at all and were squares on square. I started this work at my workrooms, but it upset the staff so much that I took six or seven of the old theatre hands down and worked at the theatre.

My brother was very fond of using Indian ink in his coloured drawings and was very particular that the material should match the drawings. At the time when 'The Vikings' was produced, the colour was not known in England and could not be dyed here, so every single bit of cloth of this colour had to be sent to Germany to be dyed there.

MOTHER'S DRESSES
Mother had to have a semi-armour dress in the first act and what she wore on her head was a bit of a difficulty. We tried two or three things which were not very successful and when it came to the dress rehearsal, Oscar Asche, who was playing the lead, refused point-blank to wear the helmet supplied to him, which was a full wig made of porcupine quills streaming back from the forehead. This was our opportunity to get Mother to wear it. She put it on and it looked splendid and she wore it, while Mr. Asche was given a much less effective headdress.

MUCH ADO AT THE IMPERIAL
Directly after 'The Vikings', 'Much Ado About Nothing' was put on by Mother which my brother also produced. Christopher St John, Penelope Wheeler and myself were in both these plays. The theatre was a beautiful theatre built for Mrs. Langtry, but it wasn't a comfortable theatre. I can never make out why that theatre wasn't nice. It was lovely to look at from the front of the house. We had rather distinguished supers. Julian Le Strange, Herbert Farjeon, Gordon Harker, Christopher St John, Penelope Wheeler and many others. Hutin Britten played the second part

146

to Mother and in one of the newspaper's entries it was said that "Miss Hutton Button played with much joie". She was always known to the company by that name afterwards.

1903-4 TOUR

Then we went on tour with 'Much Ado', 'The Merchant of Venice' 'Nance Oldfield' and 'The Good Hope', which I produced and 'The Merchant of Venice'. The production of 'Much Ado' was the same as that at the Imperial.

I well remember one Saturday night we were playing 'Much Ado' in Glasgow. In the church scene my brother's scene consisted of curtains painted with gold, dark blue, dark green, silver, tessilated and in wavy lines (three crooked Byzantines). It was the scene of the evening. The curtains hung right from the grid and looked magnificent. These curtains had to be piled at the sides ready to go up after the garden scene of a clear blue sky, which also hung from the grid. On Saturday night we found when the time came for the curtains to go up, that all the stagehands were in heavy slumber on the top of the piles of curtains and it took a long time to wake them and get them off them, which made us take a quarter of an hour more than we generally did on a Saturday night. In the old days, they used to go to sleep on the gas bags. This we didn't mind, as it used to make the gas go out with greater force and therefore made the light better.

THE MERCHANT OF VENICE

When we were playing 'The Merchant of Venice' most of the company being small part actors, went on in the Trial scene as the crowd – placed at the back of the stage. It was rather important and we all felt that we could either make or mar the scene. (I was one of the crowd) We worked very hard and after a time got a bit bored so, to vary our interest in the job, we thought that instead of the crowd all being sympathetic to Antonio, there should be a little group of the Jew's friends, so Penelope Wheeler, Charles Staite and myself, made ourselves up very Jewish indeed and I was especially successful. The three of us went into the corner of the

Court and beat our breasts and put ashes on our heads and really acted our parts very well indeed and were very pleased with ourselves and thought ourselves real little artists. In the action of the play, my Mother, who was playing Portia, after the line "Come, merchant, have you anything to say?" always walked up to the back of the stage and came face to face with the crowd. This occurs at the Jew's exultant moment and we were all being very exuberant in our joy. At that moment, my Mother saw us for the first time, and after the first look of horror, she burst forth into uncontrollable laughter – and we were paralysed and realised what we had done. All we could do was to watch the scene.

"We trifle time" says Shylock and Mother, who was convulsed with laughter, said as best she could "A pound of that same merchant's flesh is thine" and all through the next few speeches, the tears were running down her face with laughter. She then went up to the table at the back of the stage and took a law book up to consult. The Clerk of the Court, a young man who she didn't know very well, said to her in a very stern voice "Miss Terry, control yourself!" She was so furious that it stopped her.

MRS BROWN-POTTER

Mrs Cora Brown-Potter was the first American Society woman to forsake her high standing in society for the stage. Cora's marriage to James Brown-Potter in 1877 had been a prestigious one. They had one daughter, Anna who was always known as Fifi. In 1886, they visited England, traveling with a nursemaid for Anna. During this visit they were invited to spend the weekend with The Prince of Wales, who was well known to have a strong penchant for actresses.

Mr. Brown-Potter returned alone to America and Cora decided to make her career as an actress. Their subsequent divorce is well chronicled. Her letters show a devotion to her art as well as her boredom with his family, who despised anything to do with the theatre.

In 1887 Mrs Brown-Potter made her stage debut in Brighton and later that same year, started a partnership with Kyrle Bellew which lasted more than ten years.

50. Mrs. Brown-Potter

51. Mrs Brown-Potter in *Nicandra*

Together they successfully toured the world. In Australia, she exclusively endorsed Worth gowns, both on and off stage.

When she retired to the country, Mrs. Brown-Potter concentrated on gardening and a curious interest in the occult. She believed in reincarnation and claimed to read perfect sanskrit which she had never learned but knew from an earlier existence thousands of years previously!

NICANDRA
1901 In a play called 'Nicandra' at the Avenue Theatre, Willie Edwin's season, I had to make a dress (from a rough design by Cissie (Cicely) Gordon Lennox) for Mrs. Brown-Potter.

Willie Edwin said to me "I want this dress to be very seductive. We won't have the ordinary low neck but we will have it fastened right up to the neck and a three-cornered piece cut out below this, very suggestive, no sleeves at all, and large bracelets." In fact a kind of amorous dress, I gathered. When I showed it to Mrs. Potter, she laughed heartily and said "He has never seen my arms – they are like broomsticks and his little peephole would only show up my ribs." She was very very thin but had lovely line of neck and shoulder and I had made lots of dresses for her, all of which had long sleeves. Needless to say Willie Edwin's design had to be altered. I made her a suitable scaly dress of blue green sequins in which she looked rather lovely and exotic in this rather commonplace farce.

1904 DU BARRY at the Savoy Theatre
Later on I again worked for Mrs. Brown-Potter when she had a rather marvellous but disastrous season at the Savoy theatre. The play was called 'Du Barry'. It was one of the most beautiful productions from the point of view of staging that had been done for some time. I designed and overlooked all the dresses and had some of them made in the theatre and helped with the production. There were about 50 men supers who appeared in the last act. There being such a large cast there was no room for them to dress in the

theatre, so they had to dress as the revolutionary crowd in rooms which the management had engaged for them at the Savoy Hotel. A lot of the people who went to supper at the hotel must have been surprised to meet this villainous crowd coming out of the Savoy. The women, who had been in the other acts, also became part of the crowd. The men were so feeble that in despair I put them all up at the back of the stage and gave the business to the women, who used to drag on the cart with the Du Barry on it, on her way to the guillotine. One of the crowd used to climb on to the wheel and give her (Mrs. Brown-Potter) a slap in the face and Mrs. Potter was terrified each night at the thought of this terrible revolutionary who used to gnash her teeth and put on the most terrifying expression.

Re Du Barry. A very well-known producer in America said to an American friend who had seen the play in Paris "before we go any further, what is du Barry – is it a cheese?"

THE GOOD HOPE 1903-1904

My friend Christopher St John had done the adaptation of 'The Good Hope' and we opened at Margate with it. During the first week of the tour when we were doing it, when the third act was on, the scene had been a series of gruesome stories, leading up to a great emotional outburst and the audience as a rule were very much worked up. Very often we had people breaking into hysterical sobs or making slight emotional disturbances. On this occasion two things coincided in a peculiar way to almost cause a panic. A woman in the pit cried out and another woman near her, smelling burning cried out "Fire!" Then nearby a man's matchbox in his pocket caught fire, and immediately the whole audience was affected. I was sitting on the other side of a table, opposite to my Mother in this scene when it happened, and I shall never forget the disappearance of white dots (which were the faces of the audience as they appeared to us on the stage) disappeared as they turned round to look at the pit.

Everyone in the audience then said "Fire!" just as if they had all rehearsed it together. Mother leant across the table to me and said "Is it behind me?" I could hardly hear her for the din, as all the audience were talking and shouting, and I said "No" and asked her if it was behind me and she said "No". Of course we kept our places and went on as if we were just acting in the ordinary way. Then a woman in the front seats of the stalls, stood up on her seat – we couldn't hear what she said but she was reassuring us. Of course the matchbox in the man's pocket had been put out at once, but no one knew what had really happened. Then Mother went down to the front of the stage and held her arms up and reassured the audience that it was a false alarm. The orchestra were back in their places and played and the people settled down for the last act.

Poor Christopher, who had heard all this riot from a dressing room where she was waiting in a great state of nerves, asked the dresser what was wrong as she saw a lot of the audience from the pit going out. They had to pass the dressing room window. She asked the dresser and wardrobe mistress what was the matter and she said quite cheerfully "I don't think they like your play, Miss".

On another occasion Mother was ill and although we had two understudies who played Mother's parts in the other plays, but when it came to playing Kniertje, an old woman in 'The Good Hope', they refused to do it. So I was told that I must play it. I hadn't studied the part so had to learn it in the train. I knew a certain amount about it from rehearsals, but I had never played an old woman's part before. The Company were all very kind and Matheson Lang helped me to make up and Harcourt Williams, who I had a big scene with, when we came to it, played the whole scene for me. Christopher had to play the part that I played as a rule (Saart) – she also had not studied it, but told me quite confidently that she knew it, because, of course, she had written it – so as I had got my part in my hand, I gave her a cue quickly and she said "er-er" – and then the line. Although she knew the line, she didn't know how to take up a cue, so realising that she would have to play it the same night, she retired into the next room and concentrated on it for two hours and was letter perfect and cue perfect.

I was stage manager for the tour and had to get my scenery out, my clothes out and things in their places and on the first night in a new town, had to look to the changes of hand props and lighting myself, as we only had a few minutes interval between each act. Having rehearsed it on the Sunday in the lounge of the hotel, where some of the company were staying, on Monday morning I had to be down at the theatre to see to my ordinary job, which was a good thing as it didn't give me any time for nerves. I had no change of costume and having once been made up by Lang, I left my dressing room, which was at the top of the theatre and had no time with my numerous jobs to get back to it again. Christopher, although very nervous about her own job, was more nervous about me and had taken a small bottle of champagne into the dressing room to buck me up. We all got through the first act alright and then she said "Come upstairs, I have got a glass of champagne for you". All I kept saying was "Go away, I haven't time, I have got my lights to see to and my scene to change". At the end of the next act she tried again "I am sure it would do you good". I was feeling so jumpy that I sent her off with a flea in her ear. When we came to the fourth act, I had very little to do but it was a scene that I had often watched my mother do and had seen her reduce the audience to tears by the pathos of the few words she had to say, and as she had always said to me "Before you go on, always get yourself into the right mood", I was sitting at the side, trying my best to do so. The part Christopher St John was playing and that I played as a rule had been cut very considerably and in the last act was only a few lines to start the scene, instead of the long rather comic scene of the original. Imagine my horror, sitting at the side, to see Christopher come on to the stage with a flushed face and a bright eye and restore the whole comic scene as she had originally written it! The actor, who was on the stage with her, was most astonished, as he had never heard any of these long speeches before. When I came on, I was so upset about what she had done and so dissolved in sobs and tears, that I was quite incoherent – an ignominious end to rather a respectable get-through! I need hardly say that the bottle of champagne was finished – the poured-out glasses empty!

1903-4 THE GOOD HOPE

While on tour the difficulties of getting rooms beforehand. All you have to go on are recommendations from other people. When we arrived in Glasgow, I had engaged rooms, recommended by the business manager, as the ones that I had had before were let to pantomime people, who had not left. We arrived in the early afternoon in time for tea, to be asked by a gentleman in deep mourning if we would get our meals out and not come back till night, as they had had a sad bereavement and they wished to use our sitting room, which was the chief room in the house, for the funeral service. So dumping our bags and being as sympathetic as we could, we cleared out and went to the hotel where we had our dinner and then returned. Our sitting room and bedroom were on the ground floor on different sides of the passage. I always travelled with a large hamper with sheets to cover up the worst 'beauties' of the lodging-house keepers' rooms. I had Chinese shawls which I put over the sofas and cushions. I also had my own cushions and I used to stick my own Japanese prints, which I used to stick in the frames of the crayon drawings of the landladies' family portraits, and several little ornaments we had picked up at old curiosity shops on the way, which we put on the mantelpiece and my travelling clock and a row of books. I usually fixed this all up on the Sunday night before we went to bed so that we woke with a homey feeling to start the week.

I had finished my room and gone into the bedroom where unpacking took me some little time, when I had the occasion to go back to the sitting room to get a book to read in bed. Imagine my horror when looking on the mantelpiece, I found among my little treasures, a very dirty brush and comb, some curlers and a tooth brush. I went back and told Christopher and Penelope about this and they came back and had a look at it with me – we came to the conclusion that we must go carefully over the room to see if there was anything else that we objected to – and on my opening what I took to be a cupboard door, I discovered two females asleep in a concealed bed. We were so staggered that we shut the door and had a council of war in the next room and came to the conclusion that we must pack up our sitting room things as it was obviously not our room, and the next morning after talking to our landlord, whose house was very full on this 'festive' occasion, we moved out and changed our lodging.

There was a woman who lived at Redditch who used to tour round with a tent. She used to engage her actors with the idea of them being useful in putting it up. In the winter she always used to come and see Mother and Sir Henry when they toured and they were great friends with her. One day Mother asked her which were the most popular plays at the different villages she went to, and she replied "Shakespeare's because the people understand them". On one occasion a distinguished actor-producer was doing a pre-Shakespeare play in one of the universities, about which there was a great deal of highbrow talk – just round the corner, our Redditch friend was doing 'Jane Shaw', a much earlier play – about which there was no highbrow talk!

1905

At the time of the death of Sir Henry Irving, Ellen Terry was acting in *Alice Sit-by-the-Fire,* the play James Barrie wrote after *Peter Pan.* Ellen had just been told by her maid of Henry Irving's sudden death in Bradford. She went on as usual, but when she came to almost the last lines of the play "I had a beautiful husband once, black as the raven was his hair", she broke down completely and the curtain was brought down out of respect for her grief.

●

EDY   *ALICE SIT BY THE FIRE 1905*
This was the one and only part that I have ever played in a Barrie play and that was the part of Fanny which was only about three lines.

An interesting point of production:
At the opening of the first act while the two girls were chatting together on the sofa, Boucicault and Barrie thought it would be a good idea if they ate a box of chocolates. Instead of leaving it to them to do instinctively, Boucicault gave them set cues on certain words, when to eat them and it nearly sent them mad. They could have done it had it been left to them – but could not do it to order – and it was cut. He tried the same method with my Mother, who had known him when he was a little

tiny boy. I think her rejoinder on one of his directions was "6 rubbish Dot"! He left her alone for the rest of the production.

'A WINTER'S TALE' – His Majesty's Theatre – BEERBOHM TREE 1906 The only time that I ever slept at rehearsal was during Beerbohm Tree's production of 'A Winter's Tale' at His Majesty's Theatre. It was very hot and must have been in the summer as at 4 am the sun was shining through the gallery windows. Mother was resting in her dressing room. I was sitting by Beerbohm Tree in the Dress Circle and awoke to hear him saying "Can't you put more life into it? Can't you be funny?" to the poor actors who were all feeling anything but lively or funny. I said sarcastically "Why don't you use the property duck from 'The Merry Wives?" – fully expecting an outburst of rage from Tree. But he said "Good idea!" and there was a wait while the duck was fetched and a lot of complicated business arranged with it.

'GETTING MARRIED' at the Haymarket 12 May 1908

52 George Bernard Shaw

EDY   *Adelphi House*

Shaw lived at 10 Adelphi Terrace and his windows faced those of my flat in Adelphi House (which had been an old hotel which had been re-built into flats). I remember seeing the building when it was gutted and saying I would take the top flat in this sometime hotel of ill fame when it was re-built. Sometimes I did not take out my key so used to ring the bell downstairs and wait for Christopher to throw down the key to me. I used to do this very quietly because of the Shaw family sleeping in the house opposite. Shaw wrote to me and said he heard me outside and my voice was just what he wanted for the Bishop's wife in his play 'Getting Married' at the Haymarket. The play had been done, I think at a matinée, when I think Mary Rak had played the part, so I did not get the benefit of much rehearsal and only met the principals once, having rehearsed with the understudies and stage manager. I was always properly nervous and used to get paralysed over the words. It is the only play in which I have known two leading people play one part in one night. Fanny Brough, who was acting Mrs. Frazer, was taken ill at the end of the first act and Auriel Lee who was playing the Bishop's daughter had to be rushed into Mrs. Frazer's clothes and her understudy had to get into the wedding dress of Auriel Lee.

53. Pinkie and the Fairies 1909

> I shall never forget *Harry Ainsley's astonishment at seeing a perfectly strange daughter with whom he had never rehearsed – but he was quite pleased as she was very pretty. I think it was while I was there that I did my first London production. This was a curtain raiser for Charles Hawtrey at the Vaudeville. (it was a one act play). I don't think my name was ever on the programme but I got my cheque.

* Henry Hinchliffe Ainley (1879-1945), Actor

1909 PINKIE AND THE FAIRIES

> A very charming play written by Graham Robertson (see letter to Mother). In this I had to sing in a trio with two other people who could not sing – so it was alright – I played Aunt Imogen. I stood by as an understudy to Mother as she did not play twice in one day. I either went on at the matinée or evening performance whichever Mother did not play. This play had the distinction of being a very witty children's play which most children's plays are not.

CHAPTER SIXTEEN

Suffrage and the Pioneer Players

54. Women's Freedom League

EDY   1909 *SUFFRAGE*

At this time I was very much interested in the movement for Women's Suffrage. When I was a child, of course I did not realise that women were under any disabilities, because in our family the women always seemed to be the ones who did the things and when we were little, if my brother used to cry, I used to say to him "Be a woman!" as they seemed much more brave and capable than men!

Later I realised that the political weapon of the vote was necessary to remove the disabilities that some women had to endure. It did not make any difference on the stage as we received the same salaries as men and were not paid less because we were women.

I joined the Freedom League – I think it was through Cicely Hamilton – I always was given very small things to do. On one occasion I was asked by someone to take over some work for an exhibition at Princess Skating Rink that the W.S.P.U. (Women's Social & Political Union) was holding. I had promised to do a play in it 'How the Vote Was Won'. In it were Cicely Hamilton, Auriel Lee, Nigel Playfair, Beatrice Forbes Robertson, Helen Rouse. Just before the exhibition opened, Eva Moore or some other actress rang me up to know if I would take over the theatrical department, as Adeline Bourne, who had been doing it, had to give it up. I said I would. All I remember now is having loads of hatboxes full of letters handed over to me. I had no idea what the programmes were to be as there were letters for people unknown to me, saying "Darling, I will be with you at four but I must get away by six" and loads with no addresses at the head and signed only by either their Christian names or nicknames. However the little theatre which had been rigged up was always full and made a great deal of money. We had to make up our programmes every day and never knew until then what we were going to have.

THE PIONEER PLAYERS. 1911
I had been producing a lot of Pageants and plays for the suffrage and got the idea that it would be a good idea to start a society and produce three One Act Plays on Sunday evenings.

I got together a Committee and started the society called the Pioneer Players. The first programme took place at the Kingsway Theatre, 'Jack and Jill and a Friend' by Cicely Hamilton. 'The First Actress' in which Mother played Nell Gwynne and a great many star actresses were in it – and another play.

I found that I ought never to ring up a curtain myself as I made a most awful mistake in 'Jack and Jill and a Friend'. This play was divided into two halves and the curtain went down while some furniture etc had to be moved on the stage. When the curtain came down, there was a tremendous applause and I at once took up the curtain several times and things could not be got in order for the second act. I have now got a complex about taking up the curtain and always gave a signal for someone else to do it as I dare not do it myself.

'PAPHNUTIUS' 1914
A play by a Benedictine nun, translated by Christopher St. John.
This play was to take place at the National Sporting Club.
On Saturday, the day before the performance, a voluntary worker was left in charge of the office – no tickets were sold for these performances and extra tickets could only be got through members. A man came and asked for a ticket which the voluntary worker sold to him (he was a detective). As this was a private club, it endangered the licence being taken away. So I was told that the performance could not take place there. We had got all the curtain props and costumes there ready, and there was no time to let the actors know or to tell the audience of any change.

I got on to Mother and, knowing that the play which Granville Barker was producing at the Savoy was using curtains suitable to 'Paphnutius', and had an apron stage and that the theatre was near the National Sporting Club, I thought that the Savoy Theatre was the one that we must try to get. So asked Mother to ask Barker if we could have it. He said "yes" but we must get permission from H.B. Irving who had a lease on the theatre which belonged to D'Oyly Carte. H.B. also said "yes" but that she (Ellen Terry) must get in touch with D'Oyly Carte. She found that he was out of town but got a long distance call to his country home. This took about an hour and at his home they said he was out at supper somewhere, so at last I tracked him down and he gave permission. This all happened late at night and, on Sunday morning, the day the performance had to take place, of course we couldn't get transport to move the things, so we just took hand-barrows from Covent Garden Market and wheeled the things round to the Savoy and got a friend with a car to go down to Barker's in the country to ask if we might also have the theatre for a matinée on the Monday afternoon. This loan was accorded and we had a bumper house at both shows.

THOMAS BEECHAM 1909/1910/23
The first time I met Beecham was at Lady Cook's house in South Kensington – a young man and his sister were staying there and if I remember rightly, they came in to tea.

55. Thomas Beecham by EMU

*The next time I met him was at Mr. Gordon Woodhouse's. He had been asked there to meet Ethel Smyth. He was beginning to be popular and was spreading himself. After a very good dinner, Beecham and Ethel Smyth were talking and she said to V.W. (*Violet Woodhouse, wife of Gordon, a harpsichordist and friend of Ethel Smyth*) "Mr. Beecham thinks there is a chance for English opera here". Two of her operas had already been done in Germany. There was great excitement over this and Beecham was being very important. I did not like him very much.*

162

1910

The next time I saw him was at the stage door of His Majesty's Theatre after a very strenuous rehearsal of 'The Wreckers'*. He was in his shirt sleeves and was having a large tankard of beer with some of his orchestra. He had had an awful time and was happy it was over and was now enjoying himself. I liked him much better.

* opera by Ethel Smyth

Smyth's *March of the Women* was the Suffragettes' theme-song, and Thomas Beecham, who put on *The Wreckers* at Covent Garden in 1910, remembered visiting Ethel at Holloway prison, where she conducted her fellow suffragettes with a toothbrush through the bars of her cell.

1923

EDY *And when we worked together over a Sunday show for the Phoenix Society called 'The Faithful Shepherdess', we got on very well indeed, because he was such a good worker and I was also a hard worker. The only time we had a difference was when I wanted a coloratura who Herman Klein* (his pupil*) brought called Leonie Zifado. There was a great deal of talk when she was brought on to the stage and put through it and I was very anxious that she should make a slow exit singing. The moment she made a movement and took her eye off Beecham, she went to pieces. I had eventually to let her sit still as there was nothing else for it and I had to arrange it not at all the way I would have done! But we worked very well together and afterwards he wrote me a very nice letter.*

1923

In the next act, Ranalow, who was playing the God of the River, had to sing a song as the Spirit of the Fountain. He had had a lovely dress made for him. Norman Wilkinson had designed the clothes and scenery. Mrs. Lovat Fraser made the dresses and I produced it. Norman's idea of the Spirit of the Fountain was a very good idea. He had the little sticks you put in flower pots, all cut different lengths and covered with silver paper,

163

hanging from his brow and arms. They glistened and looked like running water. Knowing what the dress was like, I said to Ranelow "Keep your arms stretched out and do not move them. And when you have to lift the girl into the fountain at the end of your song, put your arms straight out towards her and I will black out."

The moment he started to sing, he started the ordinary calisthenics of a singer and stuck out like a porcupine. He then tried with the other arm and got himself worse and then he got quicker and more muddled with the song, Beecham trying to rush after him. In the end he clasped the girl, who got one of the sticks in her eye, and Ranelow, who had been concealed up to the waist in a sort of grotto, stepped out at the end of the song in – a pair of check trousers, in a fury. Beecham and I were friends over that and we were both very much amused.

BARING RANALOW 1873-1953 Irish baritone, was a member of the Beecham Opera Company.

EDY   *A DOLL'S HOUSE by Ibsen*
                 William Archer translator of Ibsen plays into English.

In the Dolls' House, Nora is eating macaroons, which her husband has forbidden and told her are bad for her teeth. The large paper bag out of which she had to eat them had always struck every actor as being very awkward, and also that it was peculiar that macaroons should be bad for the teeth.

A more enterprising producer than most, asked Archer if he were quite sure that the word really was 'macaroons' and Archer replied that he had not known what the word meant – so had put 'macaroons'. The questioner looked up the word found it really ought to have been 'caramels'.

When I was a youngster I thought very highly of him and Mother told me that he was the only critic who paid for his seat and could not be

164

influenced by the management. This may or not be true but I was very much impressed! I also met him and was rather struck by his extraordinary simplicity, when he was doing a book with Granville Barker on the National Theatre, when I was able to give him a certain amount of information about costumes in the theatre.

'ALL FOR LOVE' Phoenix Theatre
In 1922 I produced for the Phoenix 'All for Love'. Edith Evans was Cleopatra and was perfectly splendid – she worked terribly hard – she had never done anything like this part before and used to come up to my flat to rehearse.

Another time I produced Edith Evans was in 1920 at the Strand Theatre in the children's carnival. She played a disagreeable aunt and was most thrilling in the part. Sybil Thorndike was also in the play. A child who I thought would become a great actress was also playing in this play called Madeleine Robinson but I have never seen her since.

'THE CRACK' 1923 at the Apollo
At this Christmas season I produced the play and Muriel Pratt was the manageress. The cast was a good one Clare Greet, (Frank) Collier, Eric Lewis etc were in it. After they had started the season Muriel Pratt said "That song goes so well that we could have another one introduced". She said why shouldn't there be a song from the Colonel about an elephant – one of the Kipling things – and we could have an elephant which the Colonel could stalk and shoot and then it could come up behind him. She then asked "Who will do the elephant?" Most of the people were on already and the others thought it was beneath them, so Muriel Pratt said "I will do the fore legs if you will do the hind legs". And we did the elephant every night.

CLARE GREET 1871-1939 English actress
She worked extensively in films and was a favourite of Alfred Hitchcock who used her in seven of his films.

EDY   *1924 THE THEATRE ROYAL LEEDS*
I produced 'Ambush' (by Arthur Richman) with Reginald Tate in a small part and Doris Tate, his wife in the leading part. She was also very good in 'The Shewing-Up of Blanco Posnet' (Shaw) which I also produced in York in 1924.

Reginald Tate became world-famous as the first Professor Bernard Quatermass, in the 1953 BBC Television serial *The Quatermass Experiment*.

EDY   *1925 I produced a play of hers* called 'The Fog on the Moor' at Letchworth Garden City with Rose Quong and Mary Cass in the leading parts.*

* The play was written by Florence Bell (Dame Florence Eveleen Eleanore Bell DBE – See Chapter 13 'People I Knew'), who also underwrote the costs.

ROSE QUONG 1879 -1972 was a Chinese-Australian actress, performer and writer, who studied acting in England and was a very successful performer.

EDY   *NATIVITY PLAY*
1925 at Daly's Theatre for The Children's Country Holiday Fund, I produced an old English nativity play. The cast included Hayden Wright, Fay Compton, John Gielgud as the shepherd boy, Violet Tree and Elizabeth Pollock as angels, Wilfrid Walter, Valerie Taylor, Joia Tandy and Esme Pearce, Harry Oscar, Raymond Massey, Laura Cowie, Sybil Thorndike, Zena Dare, Gladys Cooper, Helen Henschel. Clare Atwood was property master. At the end of the play they had to follow the star and walk across the orchestra pit on a pair of planks and down the centre gangway. No one looked at their feet in crossing and the light was shining full in their eyes.

CHAPTER SEVENTEEN

"…And Two for Tea!"

SOME ROYAL REVELATIONS

Ellen Terry had many personal encounters with the Royal Family. She and Henry Irving were among the first actors to be summoned to Windsor and Sandringham to give Command Performances for Queen Victoria in 1889 and 1893. However, as a child, Ellen accompanied Charles Keane to Windsor. Edy's memoirs describe two enchanting incidents that have never appeared before.

EDY   *QUEEN VICTORIA AND PRINCE ALBERT*
        My mother told me that when they came to the theatre they used to bring sketching books and draw the actors. She also told me that on one occasion when she was a child, that she went with Charles Keane to Windsor Castle to play. One of the officials allowed her to pop into the banqueting room where the table was laid and she saw Prince Albert going round the table making patterns on the salt in the salt cellars

        1916 The Tea Party on Queen Alexandra's Birthday Marlborough House

EDY   *I was with Mother one day when the telephone bell went and she answered it and told me it was a message from a lady-in-waiting to Queen Alexandra (whose birthday it was) to ask her to go to Marlborough House the next afternoon. I said "Are you sure you got it right?" and she said "Yes!" so of course I had to go with her to see that she was alright and to carry her things.*

167

56. Queen Alexandra and her pet dog 1900

Accordingly we arrived the next afternoon and were met by a lady-in-waiting who said "You were not expected but the Queen will be delighted you have come" and we were ushered in to a real family party, consisting of relations. The Queen asked Mother to sit on the sofa by her and I sat somewhere near and we had tea. Queen Alexandra saying "I hope you don't mind having no saucers", as numerous little dogs were all having their tea out of the saucers. After the tea, some of the grandchildren smoked and Queen Alexandra asked me if I would. I was petrified with nervousness and said "No" to which she replied "I am very glad you don't smoke".

After tea we all adjourned to the Ballroom where the first film that Mother was ever in was shown. It was called 'Her Greatest Performance'. Queen Alexandra, who knew that Mother could not see well, walked along with her to the Ballroom trying to help her. The Queen herself had a bad knee and they were both taking hands, both using sticks which slid about on the polished floors – and Mother who always walked quickly – walked far too fast for the Queen. It must have looked a funny procession – a lady-in-waiting walking up to Queen Alexandra ready to field her – and I doing the same behind Mother.

Mother sat in the front row with the Queen to see the film and I at the back. When I came on in the film, the Queen turned round and said "That's you!" I was glad of the darkness!

Of course the mistake was that the message that the Ellen Terry film was being shown at Marlborough House on that afternoon, had somehow got mixed up. Hence our presence at the family party. My mother always made me promise that I would never divulge that she had made a mistake.

57. Edy and Ellen at the Investiture 1925

169

EDY   *1925 BUCKINGHAM PALACE*

When my mother went to Buckingham Palace to be invested with the G.B.E, (Dame Grand Cross) because of her age and bad sight, they had a wheelchair waiting for her at the lift. She was very indignant and wanted to walk of course, saying "What's that for?" but as she had a bag, a stick and a shawl and other impedimenta, I thought it was as well that she should get into the chair. I went with her as she could not go by herself. We went along miles of corridors with rather beautiful Chinese things in them that I wanted to stop and look at. At last we came to a big room where everybody else was waiting. The room was divided by a cord and they were all divided up into their places – we went right along to a closed door at the end of the room. Lena Ashwell's husband, Sir Henry Simpson* was there and he dodged under the cord and came and spoke to us – and we found ourselves in a sort of little passage room out of which there were three doors. I think the King's secretary was there who said "Come along!" to Mother. I hung on to her bag, which she was most unwilling to part with and we had a sort of tussle over it. She made me swear that I would not let it out of my hand. I was then left with her spectacles, her cloak, her shawl, her bag, her stick and my own coat and I waited outside with the wheelchair. I just saw her go in and make a most beautiful curtsey to the King and then the door shut. Then the same door opened and she came out, feeling for the doorway, then she saw me and gave me one of her horrified looks and said "Oh! I forgot to come out backwards." The King, who was rather afraid that something might happen, as after she had made two curtseys she was rather tottery, and he came to the door just behind her and heard her remark to me at which he laughed and laughed and laughed.

* Sir Henry Simpson, the royal obstetrician who was later the surgeon when Queen Elizabeth II was born;

EDY   *I had just settled Mother into the chair but was still holding a lot of the things, when the door opened again and the secretary came out and said that the King wished to see me. I was so flabbergasted that I forgot to put the things down and went in looking more like one of those music hall artists (who drop and pick up things all the time) than anything else. The King put out his hand and I curtsied and kissed his hand. Her stick went up in the air. He congratulated me on how well my mother was looking. I, thinking the interview was over, curtsied again this time dropping something. Then the King made another remark at which I curtsied again and again this was not the end, as he made another remark. So I made three false exits before I really got out. I think the King was amused as he was smiling all the time.*

Then we thought it was all over and were going home, when a message came, would we step into the next room, which was the Queen's room as she wished to see Mother. We both went in, I still clinging on to all the traps. The Queen was not at all formal and very friendly. She sat on the sofa with Mother and said she hoped that she liked the Star and she said "I had it specially made for ladies, as the other ones were too heavy to wear on women's dresses." Mother acquiesced. There was a pause and then Mother did a bit of propaganda work for the theatre. She asked Queen Mary why Their Majesties did not support the drama, to which the Queen replied. "It is so difficult because most of the plays we can't go to and those that we can go to are so dull".

When it was time to go, The Queen took Mother and helped her into the wheelchair and when the footman started to push the chair along, the Queen, noticing the fringe of Mother's shawl hanging over the wheel, stopped him and stooping down, tucked it round her feet and knees. At last we got off. Mother then said "Now what shall we do?" and insisted on going to see the pictures at the New English Art Club after which she went home, none the worse for her day's outing

1927 QUEEN MARY AT MOUNT GRACE (a pageant produced by Edith Craig at Mount Grace Priory in North Yorkshire)

EDY   *The next time I saw Queen Mary to speak to was at Mount Grace. She said "I hear that you do not live with your Mother" to which I replied*

"No, but I live next door which I think suits her better". This time the Queen was in the bright sunlight and I remember thinking that I had never seen anyone with eyes so blue!

PRINCESS BEATRICE 1934

At a theatrical exhibition at one of the big houses in Park Lane, I was taking the Princess Beatrice round – she was looking at the models, playbills and costumes. She was very interested and suddenly she said "Mama would have been so interested in all this." She looked so young that for a moment I wondered who Mama could have been, when I suddenly realised that it was Queen Victoria.

CHAPTER EIGHTEEN

Death of Ellen Terry

DAME ELLEN TERRY 1847-1928

58. Ellen Terry as The Nurse in *Romeo and Juliet* –
her final appearance on stage.

EDY   *E.T. One of the last things she said when she was very ill.*

Sometimes in her last years, she looked upon me as about seven years old and used to say some of the early nursery rhymes – one being "One Two Buckle My Shoe". The doctor at this time would not let her have what she called a good square meal. She used to say to me "Go down to the kitchen and tell them to cook me a nice chicken. This is a very nice inn and they will do it." So when she came to "Nine Ten – a good fat hen" she used to say "and I should like to have some" and she was laughing when she said it.

E.T's last word
She used to spell over and over again "H.A.P.P.Y."

The reminiscences end here.

59. Ellen Terry's funeral

Epilogue

c/o Miss Edith Craig
31 Bedford Street
Covent Garden
London W.C.2.
17th August 1929

My darling Curlington,

I really do not know how to begin this letter and I think I should like you to give it back to me as a record as I cannot possibly put all I want to in my diary. I think I will begin by telling you about the translation of the earthly remains of our dear Ellen Terry. You know that from the time she was cremated until today, her ashes have been in this flat in a little room which was made into a kind of sanctuary. With a little altar on which stood two candlesticks and on the wall behind hung a crucifix. The casket which was the work of Paul Cooper, was at all times surrounded by beautiful flowers, many of which came from her beloved Smallhythe – others from Covent Garden and other places.

Late last night Edy, Clare Atwood, Christopher St John and myself went in and Chris recited the litany to which we responded for the repose of her soul. I felt it to be a great honor [sic] to be allowed to enter into such a service as this. This morning we were up early and Edy carried the casket to the church. She had a sling to take a little of the weight – and again I was honoured to be allowed or rather asked by Edy to lift it off the altar and put it into her arms. Then at

8.15 am we entered the church, St Paul's Covent Garden, where the Reverend Hart Davis who is the Rector, took the casket and placed it on the altar of the Lady Chapel. He then performed the ceremony of the celebration (with an acolyte) to serve (I don't know what they are really called in the Church of England). Edy sat in front by herself and Chris and Tony and myself also May Eversley behind and we 3 of course could not communicate not belonging to that denomination.

After that we came home and partook of some breakfast and then did different things until 1.30 – I ought to have said that about halfway through the early celebration, the Reverend Hart Davis put the casket into a most beautiful nitch [*sic*] also designed by Paul Cooper and all the work that is done on it is done by the artists themselves, the gates, stonework and engraving which is all most beautiful and dignified – just her name Ellen Terry Actress 1848 – 1928.

60. The Casket containing Ellen Terry's ashes, St Paul's Covent Garden

After the early service, a green cloth was hung over it. At 1.15 when we entered the church, it seemed pretty well filled. Sharp and Tilly, the gardener and his wife from Smallhythe came up this morning with baskets of rosemary and before we went to the church, we each had a sprig given to us and then they took the baskets to the church door and gave it to the people who entered. Ellen Terry had a lovely bush of it by her farmhouse door at Smallhythe and she has often given me a sprig herself and said "This for remembrance" I thought it was a lovely idea and it made the church smell so beautiful. In the first pew of the two middle sections of pews sat from left to right Sir John Martin Harvey (he sat there because he was reading the Lesson), then Mrs. Gielgud, then Miss Marion Terry then Edy then Olive Chaplin or you know her as Olive Terry – in the pew behind there sat Mr Fred Terry, May Eversley, Clare Atwood, myself and Christopher – we had first of all the "Londonderry Air" which was said by a friend of Ellen's Miss Palgrave that "Lady"* had said she would like to have played at her funeral. Then we had again her 3 favourite hymns; the choir is comprised of girls and men. The girls wear a black sort of mortarboard rather like the cap they give for the LL.D degree at St Andrews. After the Magnificat had been sung about halfway through the service, the Reverend Hart Davis came from his place and Edy went with him and a warden bearing a processional cross and then Edy tore aside the curtain which was only pinned with two drawing pins. The music was beautiful and everything went with the joy and though it is a strange word to use success and one can never believe that her spirit is not taking part and helping with it all. After the service the organist played a lovely thing of Bach, a Fantasia in C minor (I believe) of which she was very fond. After that all the people filed up after Edy had taken her Aunt Marion up to see the receptacle.

* our name for Ellen Terry

A lot of photographers came and took photographs. Henry Ainley was there and crowds of other people. At 2.30 we left the church and Sir Albert Seymour came up to the flat for a few minutes. Then another man who was called Freddy and who told me himself that Dame Ellen had picked him out off the streets and he had been callboy at the Lyceum in the old days when Henry Irving and Ellen Terry were giving their wonderful performances. After he had gone, Lindsay Jardine and Nona Stewart, who had come up from Dorset this morning for the ceremony, came and had tea.

Vera Holme

61. Visiting Edy at home in Smallhythe
Vera 'Jacko' Holme, her nephew Jack Holme, Clare Atwood, Edy Craig
August 1939 Tenterden

Honouring Edy

62. Pepe on Edy's memorial stone

EDITH CRAIG, daughter of Ellen Terry, died 63 years ago on March 27th 1947 but until September 11th 2010 there was no tombstone, plaque or memorial to say she ever lived.

That was the day when my thirty celebrated guests from all over the UK, attended The Blessing and Dedication of a Memorial Stone to Edith Craig in the tiny churchyard of St John the Baptist Church, Smallhythe Kent, next to the

179

National Trust Ellen Terry Museum where Edy and her famous mother lived and died.

When Edith Craig died she left a request that her ashes be buried with her two lesbian partners, the writer Christopher St John (Christabel Marshall) and the artist Tony (Clare) Atwood. By the time they passed away in the 1960's, Edy's ashes were mislaid. Dismayed at the loss of her ashes, her two friends opted for burial and they lie side by side next to the gate leading to Priest's House where they had lived with Edy.

I have always felt that Edy's huge contribution to English theatre has long been overlooked. Since I purchased the notebook of her reminiscences, I have spent countless hours discovering more about this extraordinary woman, hours that gave me lasting pleasure as I learnt more about her, her mother and the theatre of her time. I felt I wanted to thank her, for she has filled the years of my retirement with theatrical knowledge that I would never have discovered without her. This year I decided to commission a memorial stone for Edy to be placed next to her two beloved companions.

Among the guests, two great acting families were represented – The Sindens and the Thorndikes, both closely connected with Edith Craig and Ellen Terry. Also present were Dave and Richard Brind, sons of Charlie Brind, handyman and gardener to Edy. In the notebook, I had found a copy of the Order of Service with prayers originally written for Edy's funeral in 1947. These were read by Daniel and Nina Thorndike (Dame Sybil's nephew and great-niece) and Marc Sinden, standing in for his father Sir Donald Sinden who was not well enough to attend the ceremony. I read the eulogy, a moving tribute to Edy written in 1947 by actress/producer Margaret Webster, daughter of actress Dame May Whitty. (See Coda)

After the short simple ceremony, the Revd Canon Howard Cocks, Rector of Winchelsea, blessed the stone by sprinkling it with Holy Water. The thirty guests were then each given a golden rose and a sprig of rosemary to lay on the stone, before walking through the little gate, past Edy's house to Ellen's garden next door where a Champagne Buffet Lunch was served. Personal messages from Dame Judi Dench and her actress daughter Finty Williams, Edward, Joanna, Emilia and Freddie Fox and the biographer Sir Michael Holroyd were read out by Dr. Henry Dyson of Durham University.

63. Edy in bed with her cat by Tony (Clare Atwood)

Cats were Edy's favourite pet. She adored them. They appeared with her in photographs, paintings and an article appeared in the London Evening News of February 19, 1923 describing how her cat pined for her, while Edy was filming abroad in Egypt.

At the dedication ceremony that Saturday morning, a ginger cat appeared from nowhere and entered St John's church when the thirty invited guests were gathering. When I led them out to the graveyard for the ceremony, the cat bounded ahead of me, leading the way and, out of all the gravestones in the churchyard, went straight to Edy's new memorial stone and sat on it.

There is a sad ending to this story. The cat met a violent end within two months. It was found dead under a tree. It was unmarked but had probably been hit by a car and crawled away to die in a garden.

In Chapter One, you will recall Edy's description of her first pet, a kitten who also met with a violent end. Edy gave her kitten four curious names – *Cripto Concord Syphonos Tomato.* By a strange coincidence the cat who came to the Dedication Ceremony also had four names – *Pepe Sanchez Rodrigo Gonzalez.* How strange that both cats had four names and died from a similar violent blow!

"I believe cats to be spirits come to earth" wrote Jules Verne

I often wonder if the ginger cat was sent 'on loan' by Edy to show me she was pleased to be remembered and to have her name carved in stone at last!

December 28, 2010 Ann Rachlin

64. Edith Craig 1869-1947

CODA
Tribute to Edy

BY MARGARET WEBSTER, DAUGHTER OF DAME MAY WHITTY
from "Edy – Recollections of Edith Craig"

"Edy was the daughter of a superlative actress, the sister of a man whose vision profoundly influenced the theatre of the world. Perhaps in the reference books her name will not bulk as large as theirs. She never received the public recognition that was her due. But there are very few to whom the theatre generation of today have so much cause for gratitude. She scattered the seed of knowledge and understanding with a wide and generous hand, and her plantings flower in a thousand ways that do not bear her name. I think I have never known anyone whose work, though never sufficiently recognized publicly in its own right, will go on surely, through so many people. I cannot think of her in the past tense, for even in the thought of her comes a stimulus, a sort of courage for battles yet to come. She is and always will be, alive – and working."

Bibliography

Adlard, Eleanor (editor) *Edy: Recollections of Edith Craig (1949)*

Archer, Frank*, An Actor's Notebook (1912)*

Auerbach, Nina *Ellen Terry: Player in her Time (1987)*

Bancroft, Marie and Squire *Recollections of Sixty Years (1909)*

Brereton Austin *The Lyceum and Henry Irving (1903)*

Cheshire, David F. *Portrait of Ellen Terry (1989)*

Cockin, Katharine *Edith Craig – Dramatic Lives (1998)*

Cockin Katharine *Women and Theatre in the Age of Suffrage (2001)*

Craig, Edward Gordon *Ellen Terry and her Secret Self (1931)*

Dane, Clemence *Eighty in the Shade (1959)*

Duff Gordon, Lady *Discretions and Indiscretions (1932)*

Gielgud Sir John *Distinguished Company (1972)*

Glendinning Victoria *Vita (1983)*

Gregory Eliot *The Ways of Men*

Hatton, Joseph *Henry Irving's Impressions of America (1884)*

Harbron, Dudley *The Conscious Stone –the biography of Edward Godwin (1971)*

Holroyd, Michael *A Strange Eventful History: The Dramatic Lives of Ellen Terry, Henry Irving and their Remarkable Families (2008)*

Irving, Laurence *Henry Irving: The Actor and his World (11951)*

Manvell, Roger *Ellen Terry (1968)*

Melville, Joy *Ellen and Edy (1987)*

Pemberton, T. Edgar *Ellen Terry and her Sisters (1902)*

Prideaux Tom *Love or Nothing: The Life and Times of Ellen Terry (1975)*

Robertson, W. Graham *Time Was (1931)*

Scott, Clement *The Drama of Yesterday and Today (1899)*

Shaw, Bernard *Captain Brassbound's Conversion (1899)*

St. John, Christopher *The Crimson Weed (1900)*

Shearer, Moira *Ellen Terry (1998)*

Sinden, Donald *Laughter in the Second Act (1985)*

Steen, Marguerite *A Pride of Terrys (1962)*

Steegmuller, Francis *Your Isadora The Love Story of Isadora Duncan and Gordon Craig* (1974)

Stoker, Bram *Personal Reminiscences of Henry Irving (2 volumes (1906/7)*

Tennyson, Alfred, Lord *The Cup (1881)*

Terry, Ellen *The Story of My Life (1908)*

Terry, Ellen *The Russian Ballet, illustrated by Pamela Colman Smith (1913)*

Terry Ellen *Ellen Terry's Memoirs, with a preface, noted and additional material by Edith Craig and Christopher St John (1933)*

Terry Ellen and Shaw Bernard: *A Correspondence, edited by Christopher St John (1931)*

Wolf, Virginia *Between the Acts (1941)*

Webster, Margaret *the Same Only Different: (1969)*

INDEX

of people mentioned by Edith Craig and by the
author, but excluding Ellen Terry and Edith Craig
of whom there are too many references to list
individually.